MW00887250

Off the Canvas

A Tale of Two Brothers

By

Rusty Rubin

This book is a work of fiction. Places, events, and situations in this story are purely fictional. Any resemblance to actual persons, living or dead, is coincidental.

© 2004 by Rusty Rubin. All rights reserved.

No part of this book may be reproduced, stored in a retrieval system, or transmitted by any means, electronic, mechanical, photocopying, recording, or otherwise, without written permission from the author.

First published by AuthorHouse 05/04/04

ISBN: 1-4184-6515-1 (e-book)
ISBN: 1-4184-2992-9 (Paperback)

Library of Congress Control Number: 2004092466

This book is printed on acid free paper.

Printed in the United States of America
Bloomington, IN

Chapter I

I was born during the 'Roaring Twenties' although I had absolutely nothing to do with the 'roaring' part, except maybe from my loud crying. It was 1923, almost six years to the day before the stock market crash on Black Monday, and the start of the 'Great Depression.' For those of you not familiar with history, the 'Great Depression' had nothing to do with Tony Soprano and his psychiatrist visits. Simply put, it was the greatest economic slowdown in my lifetime.

There were plenty of causes for this major downturn in our economy, triggered in part, by high unemployment and the very low (10%) stock margin rates. Folks didn't have the money to cover the shortfall when the stocks fell. The panic also created a run on the banks, some of whom had to close their doors because they didn't have enough money on hand to meet the demand.

It was a sad time in American history, with long bread and soup lines full of hungry people who had families to feed. As stock margin rates rose a few folks jumped off roofs and out of windows. But the suicides that occurred were not as many as it was made out to be. The best known song of that era was "Buddy Can You Spare a Dime". Most people would have answered 'no!. These times were very tough.

'Silent' Cal Coolidge took over the Presidency when Warren Harding died in office, supposedly during an extra marital tryst. 'Now that was a great way to go. Harding was a man who died as good as he lived', our Uncle Johnny would laughingly say, long after Harding's death.

1923 also marked the start of the Spanish Civil War, which in the end resulted in the very long regime of Generalissimo Francisco Franco, and, in boxing, Jack Dempsey was the world heavyweight champion.

The good news was that after a long no-decision contest in World War 1, the world was at peace again, thanks to the Versailles Treaty.

These were times to be enjoyed, if one could afford to enjoy them. A buck went very far in those days, and the million dollar purses for championship boxing purses today (as well as the earnings of many of our over-paid, pampered, steroid using athletes) was inconceivable. Steroids or even drug use for that matter, were largely unheard of. Booze was the drug of choice.

Prohibition was the law of the land, but you could always find a place to buy a drink if you wanted to. Bootleg whiskey was easy to come by, despite Federal Governments crackdown on 'white lightning'. I don't remember much of that, but my Uncle Johnny often told me about those days in the long-distant past.

Now, at age 80, I don't think and talk as well as I used to, and I sure don't move as quickly due to these creaky old bones, I've had a wonderful life to reflect back on. If I could go back in time, I believe that I would do it all over again, and in exactly the same way. Why? Because even when I made mistakes, and I made far more than my share, I always was able to learn from them, and learning, I figure, is what our lives should be all about.

Boxing became a major part of my life in my early teens, and thanks to it, I retired at a very young age, raised a family and was able to enjoy the fruits of my labor. Life in the ring (and out) wasn't always pleasant, but life never is. To coin a boxing phrase, 'you have to learn to roll with the punches'.

I feel badly for many of today's fighters who have no clue as to how to hold onto a buck and are often taken advantage of by unscrupulous promoters. Even when treated fairly, many of these fighters don't know the value of money. The kids today are mostly from the streets and what does a kid from the ghetto know about holding onto money?

Sure, we had plenty of managers and promoters in our day that had questionable reputations as well. But I think growing up during those hard times made the fighters of the past hungry and realized the value of the almighty dollar.

I've lived long enough to see two major disasters happen. The surprise attacks on Pearl Harbor on Dec. 7, 1941 and the World Trade Center disaster in NYC, on Sept. 11, 2001. The latter was far worse, only because the targets of our enemies rage were innocent civilians. It can in no way be justified. The Japanese only targeted our military base when they first attacked and knocked out most of our Pacific Fleet and air force in Hawaii.

Things have changed a lot during my lifetime, and I'm not convinced it's for the better. In sports, expansion and ridiculously high ticket prices to pay over-paid athlete salaries, has ruined the fan base in most sports. I for one, preferred it when there where 8 teams in both of baseball's major leagues, six teams in the NHL, and 15 rounds to determine the true World Champion in my chosen sport, boxing. Now they consider 12 rounds the test of a true champion, ***Bullshit***! You have to train to be able to go 15 rounds, to be a true champion. I really wish they would bring back the 15 rounds, but I know if they ever do it, I'll be long gone.

I think the move to 12 rounds in 1983, was purely a business move to benefit the promoters and television, and does not help the sport. The move to 12-rounders was made because some folks felt that it increased safety. I don't buy it! How many knockouts occurred in the final three rounds over the years? Very few? Why? Because both fighters are tired and just don't have the strength to land that big punch to quickly end the fight. Safety my ass! The name of the game today is like it's always been MONEY!

In most cases it was expansion and greed that caused these things to occur. In short, expansion has watered down most sports and taken away fan interest. I believe the current 12-round limit was made to help fit easily into television programming, and had absolutely nothing to do with safety. Fifteen rounds required harder training and dedication and is the test of a true world champion.

Many other important events happened during my lifetime as well, but not that much in the sports world, except for Babe Ruth hitting 60 home runs and Louis beating Schmeling, and Rocky Marciano retiring with a record of 49-0.

A big win for the free world was the Berlin Wall, built by the Russians to separate the two Germany's after World War II, and was torn down, marking the beginning of the end of Communism as a world power.

We landed astronauts on the moon, and the Cold War ended as the Soviet Union split up and the "Iron Curtain' that had fallen over much of Europe was lifted. Democracy prevailed and the world was made a far better place.

Better at least until Sept. 11, when a group of radical Islamist cowards flew two hijacked airplanes into the World Trade Center. They also flew another plane into the Pentagon, and thank God, a third that was destined for the White House in Washington DC, was forced down in the Pennsylvania countryside, by passengers on board that plane, who willingly gave their lives for their Country.

Rusty Rubin

Civil rights? Affirmative action became the law of the land, and now allows black folks to get a decent education and good jobs. Women also gained a large measure of equality with men. These are just a few good things that have happened over my lifespan. Sure, America has its problems. It's not perfect, but it's easily the greatest country this world has *ever* seen. And I'm very proud to have had the chance to have grown up and spent my life here.

One of the problems with America today is that it's no longer 'government of the people, by the people and for the people', but instead government of the people, by the rich and for the special interests. For the most part, only a person of great wealth can run for public office and have a decent chance of winning.

At age 80, going deaf, blind and bald, I don't have a lot of memories left of my early years, I can recall growing up on the outskirts of a very tough neighborhood in South Philly. But at least I lived on the 'right side of the tracks'.

One of my favorite memories was the fantastic smell of Italian home cooking on Sunday mornings, and also that I was lucky enough to be able to enjoy Christmas twice a year, once on the traditional holiday and one on the Christmas we celebrated as part of our Greek Orthodox faith, a few weeks later. Those wonderful odors as well as our always warm and friendly neighbors, make those days stand out clearly in my mind. Times were tough, but in my neighborhood of Philadelphia, I felt very secure. Everyone living there would always be around to lend a hand if one was needed. It was a true sense of community.

The best thing was that our family was very fortunate to have lived on the 'right side' of the train tracks, usually used by the long, ;loud freight trains but also used to carry passengers to various parts of the country. This was paradise as opposed to the far poorer and rougher neighborhoods on the other side. The trains ran through town fairly often and usually very slowly. I found it enjoyable to watch the gray billows of smoke and the sound of the train whistles, although at times our apartment did shake a bit when a very large freight train was slowly rumbling through.

Unfortunately for my smaller and younger, freckle faced brother Billy and I, our school was located on that South side of the tracks, and created occasional problems walking to and from classes. This was the side of the tracks that most of the hobos hung out, waiting for a chance to board the trains as they slowed down to pick up the passengers and freight, heading both East and West. The hobos never really bothered folks, all they wanted was a job and food. Simply stated, a chance to survive.

While the hobos never caused us any problems, it was sad seeing these poor, human wretches go through garbage cans or pick up and smoke cigarette or cigar butts.

It really didn't matter much, that there were some that had and far more that didn't. It's been pretty much that way all my life, although for awhile the gap narrowed and a large middle class developed in America. Now, it seems like we're going backwards. There's the very rich and the very poor. The middle class is quickly disappearing again.

In retrospect, I think that our school being on the wrong side of the tracks was really a blessing in disguise. It got my kid brother Billy and I involved with boxing. We probably would have never discovered the sport that provided our families with many wonderful things in life, as well as the great memories I am about to recount. But we didn't go into boxing for the money or the memories, we had learned for self-defense.

At that time no one knew or cared how dangerous cigarettes, pipes or cigars were, It was never a big deal, because few could afford to support the habit, because cigarettes cost something like ten cents a pack back then, maybe less. That was a lot of money then. And there was no such thing as filter cigarettes on the market either. 'Lucky Strike, Camels, Philip Morris and Old Gold were the brands of choice for those who picked up the habit. White Owl was the cigar of choice.

It was prohibition, an amendment to our Constitution that made selling alcohol illegal that meant quick money for some, and led to the rise of the gangsters that roamed the streets, selling bootleg alcohol to anyone who was interested and could afford it. And while most of the booze was sold in the back of warehouses and illegal gambling parlors, some was also sold out of the back of delivery trucks, using a different business name as a façade. Prohibition was doomed to failure and led to the rise of the gangster era.

And the mob itself created a lot of problems also, but mainly those killed were other mobsters, so we felt it was no great loss. And these guys did protect their neighborhoods, so if you lived there you were always very safe.

I saw a few mob 'hits' over the years, and it wasn't pretty at all.

Although our family never had much money, I don't recall ever going hungry. The warmth of Italian families and the smell of their home cooking on a Sunday morning is one that will remain with me till the day I die. Good pasta, it's all in the sauce. You still can't buy real pasta sauce in cans. Back then, they cooked the ingredients over night. You could eat the sauce without the pasta, just dipped in bread, and it was delicious. And, the Italian families were always very generous to us, "Tony, Billy, come on up, manga, manga" (eat, eat). It was a wonder that Billy and I never fought at heavyweight. We sure ate enough.

In those days, Billy was always by my side. As the older brother, I was obligated to take care of him, which is one of the reasons I had to remain in school instead of getting a much needed job. Many of the kids my age dropped out and sold their wares for a few pennies, on street corners to help support their families. Many of these young men had fathers who were maimed or killed in the 'war to end all wars', but didn't'.

It was sad to see so many veterans of that conflict, some without arms and/or legs, also selling items or panhandling. We didn't do a very good job taking care of our veterans in those days. Of course our government denying the deadly effects that Agent Orange had on our soldiers after the Viet Nam war, didn't do much to help the veterans or the credibility of our government either. But everyone makes mistakes.

While most folks had very little in those days, we were lucky enough to grow up around some wonderful, caring people, who shared what little they had with those less fortunate. We had block parties to celebrate certain holidays or events, which always included food, music and dancing, and everyone in the neighborhood took part. The depression may have been a harsh reality in the real world, but in our little corner, it didn't seem to exist.

Mom, Billy and I lived on the second floor of a four-floor walk-up, with two apartments on each floor and another for the superintendent in the dank basement. We had one bathroom between the apartments that both families had to share.

It was far from paradise, but we didn't know it then, and life probably was as good as most of the other folks living in North Philadelphia at the time. We always had fresh milk, lard and eggs in the (icebox) now called a refrigerator (delivered by the milkman wearing a white uniform and cap and driving a horse and cart, twice a week) and cereal and bread to make sandwiches. We had meat twice a week, except for the holidays, as that was all we could afford. But compared to many others, we were very well off.

There were very few cars on the streets then, and they all had hand cranks in the front that you had to wind up to start the engine, running boards to stand on, and rumble seats in place of what would be the trunk of today's autos. Our family couldn't afford a vehicle and mom didn't drive anyhow.

Trolley tracks and overhead power lines were everywhere and those trolley cars (open busses that ran on the tracks) were the major source of transportation. The train and bus system was just starting to be built to accommodate the growing populace.

I remember the conductors on those trolley cars, with their dark blue uniforms, always wearing a pocket watch to make sure they stayed on schedule, and they always seemed to enjoy clanging the bell whenever they stopped, to tell everyone to get on board.

The folks of today seem to have it much better, I think. If we were impoverished we sure didn't know it. At least back then the world was at peace, and because of America's distance to the other continents, we always felt perfectly safe.

11

Rusty Rubin

It was in this era of prohibition and poverty that the gangsters flourished. Folks like John Dillinger, 'Machine Gun' Kelly, Ma Barker, 'Baby Face' Nelson, Bonnie and Clyde, 'Dutch' Shultz, Al Capone and the like caused the creation of the FBI, with its first director, J. Edgar Hoover.

Although some of the mobsters lived in South Philly, they never bothered us, as most of the underworld did their robberies, etc. in major cities in the Midwest, and in far better neighborhoods. What could they get from ours? Nothing, except the resentment of all who lived here.

There were undesirables in the area where we were growing up, but I can't remember ever being spoken to by these gangsters. If I was, I didn't knew who they were and always kept in the dark about what these guys really did. Some locals looked at these gangsters as folk heroes but most, my family included, had little or no respect for them and the way they made their living. Mom would always say "Why don't they go out and earn a decent living working hard like everyone else?" Of course mom didn't seem to realize that not 'everyone else' could find jobs at that time.

In the real world, the Charleston dance craze was going out and the 'Big Band' era was coming in, and I still love that great music. Glenn Miller was my personal favorite, but he sadly died in a plane crash during WWII. Mom and Uncle Johnny loved Al Jolson. And Harry James played a great trumpet, and we could always "Swing and Sway with Sammy Kaye". Guy Lombardo had his "Royal Canadians" and Frank Sinatra was just starting out on what was to become a fabled career. Real music in those days made life worthwhile.

Burlesque was the rage, but I only went there once, with Billy, when we were older and single. I guess it was fun, but we didn't enjoy it that much. I guess our moral Christian upbringing had something to do with it.

We would bring hard, wooden folding chairs to the movies, where they charged a nickel to get in (sometimes we sneaked in to save the money when we could). But we did prefer the movies to the burlesque. Forgive me if I'm slightly off on these dates, they just seem to run together in my mind, at this juncture of my life.

The thing that I remember was having to dress up to go to church on Sunday, with my mom and Billy. It wasn't going to church that bothered me, but in truth, I hated having to wear suspenders, a sport jacket and bow tie. And having to shine Billy's and my shoes could also be a royal pain in the ass. But it was a weekly ritual for me and I had to do it. That was a job mom assigned to me.

Billy could shine his own shoes, but really didn't get them as spit-clean as mom liked. He never seemed to mind dressing up and going to Church though. At that time he always seemed to be more into the religious aspect of life than I was. Uncle Johnny and Aunt Jen also joined us on every Sunday, making it a 'family day' so to speak.

13

Still, times must have been hard because I can recall raggedy street venders selling foods out of pushcarts and while most of the customers were there to look, a few came to buy and more than a few came to steal. I'm sure it was out of necessity as money was scarce to say the least. Not that it made stealing right, but at least it was understandable. Eat or starve, life in those days was that simple. And no one wanted to starve.

My memories remain pretty vague, but I recall seeing the open back ice truck, the driver cutting up blocks of ice on the back of it, with his ice pick and delivering them to his customers wrapped in a brown burlap sack. On hot days, he would give some ice chips to us kids to suck on. If refrigerators were invented back then, we certainly didn't have one. We used an old cream colored icebox, which looked somewhat like a refrigerator does today, only smaller, but used ice to keep our perishable foods cold and fresh.

Once a week, a guy with a white and blue pushcart visited the neighborhood. He was selling ice cream bars from a frozen section of his cart for five cents. That too was a treat we always enjoyed when we could afford it.

Then there were the neighborhood mom and pop grocery and candy stores, almost unheard of today, taken over or forced out of business by the big corporations and supermarkets. But the candy stores had counter seats, booths and juke boxes and were fun to hang out in. It's sad that they call what we have today, progress.

I vividly recall the old coiled, silver colored radiators, and long heating pipes of the same color, which may can be found in many of the older homes today. There where the trucks with their long cylinder chutes pouring heating coal into the basements of homes, which were shoveled by the building superintendent into the furnace. We didn't always have heat to keep us warm, but we always had plenty of hand-me-down sweaters that were given to us by relatives or friends, or from church members, like much of our clothing, little was purchased new.

I remember another old guy with a pushcart who always bought or sold rags, yelling out in some strange language I never understood. Looking back, I have no idea why he did that or what he said, but it was the Depression Era and money was short and times were hard. Maybe the rag guy of the past would become the 'thrift store' owner of today.

In those days we had the family doctor, who, unlike today, never refused to make house calls when you called him on your crank-up telephone. The phone was something mom said we needed close by in case one of us kids got sick. How many doctors make house calls today? Better transportation and bigger and hopefully better hospitals have made that also, a thing of the past. That's sad. The family doctor was not just a physician, he was a friend. The family doctor was a specialist in everything. And for what it's worth I have to add that I absolutely have no use or respect for HMO's. Their only interest is the bottom line, money, and not the health of their members.

Unlike today, family was very important. We ate dinner and got together on the holidays. This was a must, for food, laughs, and on rare occasions, presents. Uncle Johnny got Billy and me, our first set of boxing gloves one Christmas, and we would spar with each other constantly. It was a great outlet for our frustrations. Billy, although smaller, always seemed to hit harder, even then.

Mom didn't like the idea of the gloves. She wanted Uncle Johnny to take them back and buy us something safe to play with, or better yet, warm clothing. She hated the idea of having her sons go to school or church with a black eye, but she was always prepared to treat the injured eye with a raw steak, or ice, as well as a bloody nose with cotton balls. Unlike Uncle Johnny, mom was never a fan of 'the violent sport of boxing'.

Mom, may she rest in peace, was a very special lady. In our eyes, she was nothing less than a Saint. Nothing stopped her from going to work and earning the money needed to raise us. I remember her with dark hair, streaked with gray, put up in a bun in the back and glasses strung around her neck. She had blue eyes which she usually covered with small framed reading glasses. Mom also had false teeth which she put in a cup, with some type of powder, for cleaning when she removed them a night. She needed a hearing aid, but could never afford one.

Despite her sometimes-frail health, mom always had a big smile on her face and a warm, open hand, for anyone who needed a helping hand. She believed in peace, and to her boxing was quite the opposite. But she never put boxing down. She would say that 'at least it's an honest way to make a living'. Honest? Most of the time I found it that way, but that was to be years in the future.

Most of all, what stands out from those long ago times past, was being constantly picked on when away from the safety of our home. Those who had (I think my family was one of the lucky ones) were always in danger of being robbed by the have nots. And there were far more of them than us. Jobs and money was scarce. Some folks had to walk around with holes in the soles of their shoes because they couldn't afford to have them fixed or buy new ones. But holes or not, almost all the neighborhood folks, always seemed to make church services on Sunday, at least those who were of our faith. And those in the church that had, made sure that those who didn't, were taken care.

That was when I was about seven years old. I was fairly big for my age, but certainly not big enough to stand up against the roving street gangs who would literally strip the clothes off your back, because they had few of their own. There were usually too many so I couldn't fight back and I was far too slow to even attempt to run away. It was usually three (or more) against me and sometimes Billy (who was much too small to be of any help then), and what did I know about self-defense? Not much, maybe less!

Franklin Delano Roosevelt became our President in 1932, replacing Herbert Hoover, who many blamed the Depression on. FDR was in his first of almost four full terms in office. When you consider that he had to solve the economic problems of our times and then having to deal with WWII in his fourth and final term of office, it was obvious that he had to do a yeoman job.

Mom voted for him because he promised to get America out of the depression. But in truth, she would always vote Democratic. She believed that Democrats were good for the poor folks in America and Republicans only cared about money, a theory many people still support today. Personally, I have always voted for the candidate not the party.

My dad, Spiro? I don't remember him at all. He left home shortly after I was born, or so they tell me, and recently I learn that although he deserted his family, he had joined the Army, and had become a war hero, a high ranking officer who was killed in France during World War II.

I have a non-wedding picture of him in uniform that mom somehow got her hands on. I still carry it in my wallet. His name was Frank and he was a fairly burly, good looking guy. He looked very young when the photo was taken.

The military gave mom a 'Purple Heart' for dad's courage under fire, but since he had deserted us, she accepted it grudgingly, but refused to keep it and then turned it over to dad's younger brother, Uncle Johnny, who never spoke of dad, to us anyway.

This medal for heroism is now in my possession, and along with the photo, it will be given to my grandson when I pass on. No matter how dad may have treated his family, he was our father, and served his country with honor.

I had a younger (by two years) brother, Billy. He was much smaller than me, with curly red hair, dimples, freckles and brown eyes, while my hair was straight, slicked back and brown, and my eyes were blue-green. When he was young, Billy was very quiet and seemed insecure. But circumstances forced him to change his demeanor quickly.

Since most of the neighborhood kids either worked or went to school, there was little time for sports in our lives, so days were pretty routine. Get up, wash, get dress, slick down my hair, help groom and dress Billy, and go down to a hot breakfast of cereal and milk, (bacon and eggs was always a treat) which mom always had ready (prepared along with sandwiches in a brown paper bag, and a small container of chocolate milk, for school lunch) before she left for work.

The thugs would often steal our lunches. At one point I asked mom not to make them anymore, because that made Billy and I easy targets for these punks. But mom insisted that we take our lunch, but not fight over it, and on the rare days that we weren't robbed of them, the sandwiches did go down real smooth.

And it was because mom had to work to earn a living (she was a cashier in a local department store, before being laid off a few years later when it closed) that I had to remain home and take care of Billy. Other kids in the neighborhood used to stand on street corners and sell their wares, some sold apples for a penny apiece. I wanted to do that to help out, but mom wouldn't hear of it. "Someone has to take care of Billy. He's too young to take care of himself, and Uncle Johnny and Aunt Jen shouldn't be burdened", she would say.

Because of my obligations to Billy, I never worked, although sometimes I asked mom if I could leave school and try to find a full time job to help financially. She'd never let me. A good education and taking care of Billy was most important thing in her eyes. So mom was the only breadwinner, although she could always count on Uncle Johnny for financial help if needed. I doubt he ever said 'no'. Mom would never miss the trolley cars that would take her back and fourth to work. And she never did tell us who Billy's father was, no one asked and we never found out. I think it really mattered to Billy, because he mentioned it a few times. We asked Uncle Johnny but he said he didn't know either.

School? Well, it wasn't our grades that caused us trouble, school was also a safe haven for us. The problems were the street bullies we had to face when walking to and from the small school, but not in the classroom itself. Although the halls of the school seemed to be a good place for them to grab us for a 'shakedown', as there was no security, it rarely happened. Home and school were the two places where we seemed to be always safe.

On the mean streets, we were never safe, but felt at ease when one of the three foot-patrol policemen was nearby, blue cap and uniform and always swinging his brown billy-club on a leather strap. Unlike many of the kids of today, we knew and respected the beat cop. We knew these guys were our friends, and would keep us safe, if they could. Sadly there weren't enough of them to patrol everywhere. And there was no money to add any more police to the payroll. Maybe that's why you rarely if ever see a beat cop anymore.

I may have been big, but I was never fast. I always got picked on a lot. When I was with Billy, I had to protect him, and more often than not I'd wind up with scrapes on my elbows and knees, a bloody nose, cut lip, and usually we both went home crying.

Scared? You bet, but what choice did we have? When it was just one member of the gang, or an individual that jumped us, I was usually strong enough to hold my own and allow Billy enough time to run home. I won my share of

Rusty Rubin

one on one contests, but when there were two or more thugs, which was the rule, I had absolutely no chance.

Although mom didn't like me fighting, she knew I had an obligation and responsibility to protect Billy, and I'm not convinced that having to constantly repair or replace my torn clothes was not a major factor in shortening her lifespan. Everything was much cheaper then, but that doesn't mean that they were affordable. Most of the time, they weren't.

I remember our Uncle Johnny, dad's younger brother who was like a father to us, and who lived just a few blocks away. He was always listening to the old light brown, rounded Philco radio he had, and he was a great sports fan. Baseball and boxing were the loves of his life, (even more so than my Aunt Jen, his wife, I often thought). I never once heard him say a negative word about anyone who had the courage to get into the ring and fight one on one. "Boxing, now that's a real man's sport. You need balls to get into the ring. Unlike baseball, it's a pure one on one sport," he would always say.

Jen? She'd listen to the radio a lot, mostly comedy shows like Fred Allen, Jack Benny and Baby Snooks.

Johnny was once a pretty fair boxer, to hear him tell the stories, but even without him acknowledging that, you could tell by the scar tissue over both his blue-grey eyes and his large nose and cauliflower ears that he had seen his share of ring action. Somehow, he had managed to keep a lot of his earnings from boxing and working in the coalmines, because at this time, he never had to work. He had developed a slight cough from the mines, which would gradually get worse, and ultimately take his life.

Football had not yet reached popularity. So whenever there was a Pittsburgh Pirate baseball game or a Friday night boxing match on the radio, Johnny would make us sit with our ears glued to the Philco. Johnny listened intently, glasses high on his forehead biting away at an old chewed up Dutch Masters or White Owl cigar that I don't remember him ever lighting.

It wasn't till much later on that I found out why a guy from Philly would become a Pirate fan. It was because Johnny was born and grew up in Pittsburgh, and had worked long and hard in the coalmines there and in Scranton and Wilkes Barre.

We didn't know it then, but Johnny had black lung disease, picked up by the coal dust in the mines. He must have known it, but never told us. Still it never changed his ever-even temperament. He had learned to 'roll with the punches' that life had tossed his way.

Aunt Jen was always very quiet. Accepting her lot in life without complaint, and we saw little of her, except at Sunday church services and holidays, and of course when we visited Uncle Johnny. She was very slender, about ten years younger than Johnny, with thinning gray hair and blue eyes. I imagine she was quite a looker when she was younger.

Like the refrigerator, I don't recall when we got our first TV. But it certainly wasn't a color set. I don't even remember when the color sets came out, I guess some time in the fifties. But I remember uncle Johnny glued to that black and white Dumont, as well in later years, watching baseball and boxing, as he had a television set long before we could afford to buy one. His was black and white. They were all black and white in those days.

Billy and I went to Johnny's apartment at times to watch the fights and partake in the cookies that Aunt Jen would always bake for us. Neither of us liked baseball much so we never spent much time watching them and as I recall they weren't on that much anyway.

The clothes washing was done in the bathtub, by hand and a scrub-board which looked like a flat accordion, and hung on the outside clothesline, except in the winter or bad weather, when we hung it anywhere in the house that we could find. Small items were placed on top of a metal tray, we placed on top of the radiator to dry.

Uncle Johnny had an old RCA Victrola (now upgraded and known as a CD player or boom box) which had a picture of a dog on it, and the words 'his master's voice'. It had an oval contraption at the end of the handle where the needle would be placed. And we didn't have CD's or 45-rpm records, just the 78 rpms. And mom loved opera, big bands and show music. No one had heard of rock and roll or rap. At Uncle Johnny's, it was always folk or country music.

The kids of today will never understand or appreciate what real music was. Then again, I don't understand what the kids listen to that passes for music nowadays. I guess different times bring different cultures. I've always believed in live and let live, and never forced anyone to listen to the music I enjoyed. Today they blast the volume and far worse, the base, so everyone around is forced to listen to something they may not enjoy. Why they aren't told to stop or fined for disturbing the peace, is beyond my comprehension. It's downright rude!

Personally, I think music that preaches sex and drugs and violence, particularly against women, is sending our kids the wrong message, and shouldn't be allowed. But heck, I'm 80 years old, writing this book, and thank God we still have something called 'freedom of speech'. It's hard to argue with that. But no one is forced to read this book, or are forced to listen to kids blasting that noise called music today.

I remember Uncle Johnny was always talking about his favorite fighters, Pittsburgh guys and other greats like heavyweight champion Joe Louis, Billy Conn, Archie Moore, Harry Greb, Charley Burley, Fritzie Zivic, and his favorite; a Penn State collegiate boxer named Billy Soose. Of course, all but Moore, Robinson and Louis were from the Pittsburgh area.

I was surprised to learn that Johnny, although he loved the big bangers, also liked Burley, even though he was never considered a big puncher. 'That man could flat out box anyone's ears off', he would always say. Johnny used to say that he hoped that someday Burley would finally get his shot at the great "Sugar" Ray Robinson, and he would out-box the pants off him and become the next middleweight champion of the world. It never happened. Robinson wouldn't fight him. "He was scared shitless of Burley", Johnny said.

Uncle Johnny was unable to work and was now living on his savings, pension, and borrowed time. Still, he accepted his fate without complaint and although he coughed a lot when talking, and used the gold spittoon by the side of his chair, he never would talk about this, or if he did, we certainly never heard it. "Death is an integral part of life," he would always say. "I know that I'm going to be going to a far better place".

I also found out after his death, that as I had suspected, Johnny had fought a few amateur and pro bouts before he began earning a living by working in the mines. Johnny always had the highest respect for those who had the courage to enter the ring and fight his opponent one on one. "Boxing is a pure sport," he used to say, "And it builds character. Boxers are the finest folks in the world." He implied that he could have continued boxing, but was guaranteed far more money by working in the mines". It was that guarantee that caused Johnny to give up what he called 'a promising ring career' and ultimately cost him his life.

It was one warm Spring day, and I was eleven years old, (I remember the year, 1934, because gangster John Dillinger was shot and killed by Federal agents outside the Biograph movie theater in Chicago). Billy and I were walking home from school when six older guys surrounded Billy and me. No one was bigger than me, but there were far too many to try and fight, and since we were completely surrounded, we had nowhere to run.

They took all our money (small change now, but a lot in those days) and the only warm jackets we owned, and told us that in the future, we'd be giving them our money whenever we saw them. We obviously had no choice, but it sure didn't feel good to be stepped on, and both Billy and I were very angry and wanted to fight back. The big question was how? They may have needed the money, but these punks could have gotten a job or found a better way to earn a living than bully younger guys who they made sure they out-numbered 3-1.

The real reason that we turned to boxing however, was not just because of the gangs, who seemed to be everywhere. It was because of just one, burly guy, who didn't seem to be very bright, a classmate unfortunately, named Morris Winston. Morris wasn't very interested in school, or hygiene. He probably never showered as he always smelled of sweat, and seemed to be so heavy, at least to Billy and I, he probably could have been a football player or sumo wrestler today.

I don't think Winston, who always wore a Philadelphia A's baseball cap to cover his crew cut, was a member of any gang. He sure didn't look like he needed any help to rob or push anyone around. And while no violence ever took place in the school, after class Morris always seemed to find a way to corner us and demand more money than we had, and always took what we gave him saying that he wanted more next time.

That routine changed one fall day, when Morris caught us in the school bathroom and announced that he would no longer accept the small pocket change that Billy and I had brought, he wanted more money and threatened to kick our asses after school. After he left, I told Billy that when school let out, to leave by the back door, run home and get Uncle Johnny or a cop, while I would try to reason with this ugly, overgrown, brainless, unkempt slob.

Billy did just that, but by the time he got back with Uncle Johnny, I had a bloody nose, two black eyes and a cut lip, my dungarees were badly torn and I had scrapes on both my arms. I was very, very sore for a few days.

I guess it could have been worse, if a group of older school kids didn't pull Winston off me, and if I didn't remember what Johnny used to always say when Billy and I were sparring, jab, jab, and jab. It was probably the jab that allowed me to land the first blow, but sadly that was the only blow I recall landing. I knew I caused some damage by the blood flowing from Winston's nose as he charged head down towards me. Thinking back I should have kicked him in the balls or teeth, but I wasn't thinking, just fighting for what I thought was my very life.

"I'm going to kick your ass, mother fucker," Winston yelled as he grabbed me and threw me roughly to the hard, cold ground.

Winston just wouldn't play fair because he wouldn't box with me. He gained the advantage when he decided to use his bulk to lunge and wrestle me to the ground, where he could hold my hands and use his hands and knees. It was like being tied up, and fighting back against this huge mass of stupidity was useless. At least I felt mentally good afterwards because I wasn't scared and was able to stand up to the school bully and actually cause his nose to bleed.

Johnny patted me on the back on the way home, telling me how proud he was of me. And that I had defended our family honor. Unfortunately, mom felt quite the opposite and grounded me for a few weekend days. All I was allowed to do was to go to school, church services on Sunday, and watch Billy if he wanted to go outside. But I couldn't help but wonder if she would have acted differently if it was Billy who had been attacked and I was protecting him by fighting back. Uncle Johnny tried to come to my rescue, with mom, but she shut him up in a hurry by saying 'Johnny, it's none of your business'.

So I suppose that it was because of our Uncle Johnny's interest in boxing and the fact that Billy and I were very easy 'targets' for the neighborhood bully's that caused us to join the local gym. Neither of us really knew or cared about what it would take to become a fighter. We didn't think of the sport as a future career. We were just sick and tired of being picked on and wanted to learn how to fight back. And in truth, it felt good knowing that I was able to make Winston bleed. That I wasn't scared of him any longer, and that suddenly it seemed that most of the kids in our school respected me.

Of course the school Principal, who didn't approve of fighting heard the story, and sent for both our mothers. Winston's mom didn't say much, and didn't look much like a rocket scientist anyway. And mom, obviously wasn't very pleased when I was suspended from all classes for two days. But in the interest of safety, mom had Billy stay home with me.

Billy and I weren't interested in the money or glory as most young men of the day, who laced up the gloves, were. We were mainly interested in learning self-defense. But we also knew that the money, at least the money that the boxers who competed at the top level were making, could help us to vastly improve our lives. But getting to the top, to us, seemed to be nothing more than a far away dream, and nothing more. And it was a dream that we almost didn't come to realize, when we found out how much time and effort it would take to become a fighter.

So one day, shortly after my confrontation with Winston, Billy and I decided to take a walk over the short distance from school to the neighborhood gym. There was an acrid, foul smell of sweat that we couldn't help but notice even before we opened the front door. "Worse than Winston," I thought. It took us a few seconds to look at each other and be absolutely sure that this was what we really wanted to do, but we took a deep breath, grabbed on to the handrail and walked up the long flight of wooden stairs to the gym itself.

We heard the constant loud clanging of a bell, and the machine gun like noises of the gym members present who were hitting the small speed bag. We saw a couple of guys boxing with headgear on, in one of the three rings that the small gym contained. The only lighting besides the glass or plastic skylight, was a light bulb that hung loosely over each ring, as well as hanging in the shower, and a small un-shaded lamp sitting on the gym managers desk.

I don't recall the type of music it was, but there was always music playing from a loudspeaker or radio, somewhere near the ring. Probably some type of Charleston or rag (dance) music, which was all the rage at the time, along with the big bands of the era, which were quickly growing in popularity, and soon would be the 'in' thing.

The gym owner/manager Paulie Reid, sat at an old, sweat stained, light colored, warped wooden desk. He was the head honcho of the South Street Gym, which was about four blocks from our home, He started to laugh

31

loudly when he first saw us. "You guys should be in kindergarten. You are way too young to fight pro and we have a policy not to allow any amateurs to train in this place. Okay, what are you kids selling today?" he asked, with a smell of whiskey on his breath, looking at Billy and smiling.

Paulie was a pretty big guy with plenty of wrinkles, and a big red nose, so I figure he must have been in his 60's, His cauliflower ears proved that he had his fair share of fights, but he did have a warm smile to go with that gruff appearance. He spoke to us with a slight Southern accent, but a nasal tone in his voice indicated an East Coast heritage. He also was bald and very badly in need of a shave.

Billy shrugged his shoulders in response, saying "Mister, we ain't selling nothing."

"Then what are you kids doing here? To watch? We don't allow that. It's against our policy." Paulie stated.

"Maybe, ask my brother, Tony". Billy turned towards me.

Paulie then turned his head towards me. He was a tall, heavyset guy, with bushy eyebrows, and was wearing a badly stained blue sweatshirt, stained heavily with armpit sweat, so it was obviously very well used. Paulie's red face looked like he had gotten too much sun. He also had a heavy growth of a beard on his face, which we were to later learn that he always had. "Okay,

Tony," he said looking a bit more serious and turning to me, "How old are you and what are you guys up to? The gym isn't a good hangout for young kids. No gym is!"

To be truthful, Paulie seemed to be somewhat intimidating and I was a bit scared, and I suddenly didn't feel like going through with it. I knew mom would never give her approval, but I looked at Billy, thought immediately about my responsibility towards him, and immediately knew what I had to do.

"We're not selling anything," I said while trying to sound extra-tough. My name is Tony Petrovic and this is my kid brother Billy" I said loudly, extending my hand and trying to act adult enough to impress him. I'm 13 and Billy is 11". I was really 11 and Billy was 9, but we were both pretty big for our ages. "We want to learn how to box like our hero, Fritzie Zivic". It was a name that Uncle Johnny used a lot, and although I can't remember ever seeing Zivic fight at that time. I tried trying to make it sound legitimate, but Paulie saw right through me.

"Fritzie Zivic, huh?" he grinned. "Have you ever seen Fritzie fight? He's a dirty fighter who lives a day to day existence. But he's always there when you need him to fight, sometimes even on a one-day notice. And he always gives one hundred percent. Have you ever been in the ring before? You know boxing can be a very dangerous and demanding sport." I knew right then that Paulie was on to us, but I still had to go through with the bluff if we were to have a chance at training here. It was the only gym within walking distance from our apartment.

"We've heard a lot of Zivic's fights on the radio," I lied. "Billy and I have had our share of street fights and we can hold our own". The truth was that the only way we ever won a fight was when I fought one on one, which seldom occurred or by out-running the bullies, which almost never happened. But I sure wasn't about to tell Paulie that. It was a bald faced lie, but I was hoping that the lie would allow us to start winning fights against the bullies.

"Well kids," he said, scratching his scraggly chin whiskers, "let me tell ya, fighting in the streets is much different than fighting in the ring. But we've got some pretty good fighters here who can help teach ya. I'll break one of my own rules. I'll let you train here. Since you're so young, it'll cost you five cents a visit, can you afford that? You'll need to be here at least three times a week. And you must stay in school and get good grades. You must be always ready to show me proof that you are doing that.

"And, from time to time, promoters come by offering money for our fighters to fight pick-ups. You aren't allowed to take any fights until I tell you that you're ready. Violate that rule and I'll throw your asses out of here for good!"

Billy and I looked at each other, knowing we couldn't afford the money, particularly since we were being robbed on a regular basis. That must have been obvious to Paulie as well, as he rubbed the back of his hairy fist against his nose and tried to decide what he should do next.

Paulie obviously sensed our situation immediately, and smiled. "Look, if you can't afford it, there's always the P.A.L. (Police Athletic League) or the local YMCA, and they don't charge anything. I run a business and I can't afford to put up any charity cases here. Word gets out and every kid in the neighborhood will be banging at my door."

Paulie could tell by the disappointed look on our faces that the P.A.L. and the YMCA, for whatever the reason (not walking distance from our home or school) was not a viable option for us.

"Tell you what, he said, rubbing his beard again, "I need some help cleaning up this place at night. I'll let you train here for free if you can lend a hand. I might even pay you a few cents if you do a good job. **B**ut you must remain in school, that's the one thing that I am going to insist on. And tell your folks not to worry, I'll make sure that you get home safely whenever you leave here. And you're not to tell anyone about our little deal, okay?"

Billy must have sensed the same relief and excitement I did, because we just looked at each other and smiled. "Mr. Reid", I said, "when can we start?"

"Call me Paulie and you can start right now if you want to!" Paulie smiled. "But first I need you to tell me your real names and ages and where you live.

Oh, and one more thing, you'll hear a lot of cussin in this place. I don't want to ever hear you using cuss words, here or on the streets."

We agreed, then picked up a pencil and truthfully filled out the back of some sort of a used index card that I guess registered all the information that Paulie needed to allow us begin our training.

We handed him the old cards, which he readily accepted and read. "Do ya folks know that you're here today?" he asked, "the truth now".

"We only have a mom, and she works most all the time. She doesn't like boxing so I don't think she'd approve of us being here," I said. "But I'd bet our Uncle Johnny would like the idea. And he's the one who always looks after us during the day. He used to box and loves boxing. You can talk to him if you want to."

Paulie shrugged; "Johnny Petrovic? I don't remember that name. Okay, but I won't call him just now, just write down their names and addresses and if they have a phone, their phone numbers, in case something happens so I can contact them. Just a friendly warning kids, becoming a fighter takes a lot of hard work and discipline. It's a very tough life. You have to be hungry and want to win badly, and right now you just don't look very hungry to me."

We didn't understand his meaning and I just shrugged "We're not, sir. We just ate our lunch in school".

Paulie roared with laughter. "OK kids, do ya own any boxing gear?"

"We have gloves," I responded, but if you can give us whatever else we need, we'll work it off. I promise. Billy and I are very hard workers. You won't be disappointed, Mr. Reid. I promise".

Paulie hesitated. "Oh what the heck? Sure, why not?" But the sneakers will probably be way too big for you". He glanced at the watch on his wrist, "but it's getting late now. What time can you be here tomorrow?"

"We'll tell Uncle Johnny and be here right after school lets out. About 2:30."

Paulie rubbed his chin thoughtfully, then shook his head. "Why don't you show up here first thing on Saturday morning instead, and we'll get one of our pros to start working with you. I'm sure we have some extra headgear, and hand-wraps, but we don't supply the mouthpieces or cups".

"We have sneakers, Mr. Reid, that's no problem, but they do have a few holes in them." I don't think we have any mouthpieces but Mom has plenty of cups at home. She says that we're much too young to drink coffee though."

"Not the right kind of cups", Paulie said with a wide, toothy grin. "Bring the sneakers, it's better than getting blisters with the larger ones. We'll see if we can get you handwraps, a mouthpiece and a protective cup. Can you be here at 9AM?"

"You bet!" Billy and I yelled in unison.

To say we were excited would not come close to the truth. We really felt like big shots as we walked slowly home. The sense of confidence that only comes from knowing that instead of being picked on, from now on we would be respected. And that was the first time that either of us could remember that we had ever felt that good. But we had to be careful so that the confidence would not turn to arrogance.

But despite Paullie's warning, we had no idea of how demanding boxing training would be for us. or how much work we would have to do to be able to compete at a top quality level, but we struggled and we survived. And no one has ever said that success comes easily.

It was a humid, rainy day that Saturday when we returned to the gym. It was the kind of a day that you could sweat your ass off just by walking the few blocks to the gym because the air was very heavy with moisture. We knew by the smell in the air that the rains would be coming very soon. But Billy and I didn't mind it at all. We were finally going to learn to be able to fight back, to defend ourselves, and that was worth all the sweat and effort we had to put into it. It wasn't going to rain on our dreams, not now, not ever.

It was a little after 9AM when we got to the gym, maybe ten minutes past the hour. To us it meant nothing, but Paulie, was just livid. He wore the same (or it looked like the same) colored sweatshirt that he had on the first time we saw him, and by the look on his beet red face, you could easily tell that he wasn't very happy with us at all.

"If you kids can't make a one hundred percent effort to make it here on time, then don't even bother ta show up and waste my very valuable time. This ain't no kid stuff. Ya gotta learn discipline. Make a mistake and fuck up in a match and ya can get hurt and maybe even lose der fight or even worse." We didn't bother to ask what the worse, was. We had a pretty good idea.

We weren't used to the cursing that we always would hear at the gym, but we didn't feign shock. We had heard a lot of that kind of talk after school, and going to and from classes, but never at home.

"You kids have got ta learn some serious discipline. Without that you'll never get anywhere as a fighter. As punishment, I want ya to get out the mop and scrub bucket in the closet (pointing) and clean up in the bathroom including the sink, toilet and the shower. Make sure you don't come out till it's so clean I can see my reflection on the tile floor".

We felt pretty depressed. It certainly wasn't what Billy and I had expected, which was to work out and learn to protect ourselves. As we looked at Paulie and then at each other, Paulie shook his head, seemingly frustrated. "Look, you kids can either do as you're told or find yourselves another gym to go to. I'm a very busy guy. I don't have the time or patience for your damn kid's games. I teach strict discipline here. You will follow and respect all my directions or you're out of here. If you can't handle it, take off now." (We later came to find out that Paulie Reid had been a drill instructor for the Army in World War 1).

Without another word Billy and I picked up the mop and scrub bucket and proceeded to clean the bathroom and showers so that it were as close to sparkling as we felt that they could get, which, due to their poor condition, really wasn't very much. When we finished Paulie inspected the work we did, nodded his approval and still sent us home, telling us to return the following Saturday, on time! We did! We certainly never wanted to get Paulie mad at us again.

Chapter II

It was 1939, Billy and I had been going to school to learn and to the gym to workout on a regular basis. We were now dedicated and determined to become professional prize fighters.

The 'Brown Bomber', Joe Louis had beaten Jimmy Braddock to regain the heavyweight title that he had lost to Max Schmeling in 1936, and Louis had then become a hero to all Americans. That was because Schmeling was (as we came to find out years later, erroneously) a Nazi. For a black American to beat an Aryan was a cause for great pain for Germany and great patriotism at home. Because Lewis was a Negro, he helped unite the country at a time when prejudice was running rampant, particularly in the deep South.

Paulie paid off a friend of his to alter the dates on our birth certificates, to make Billy and I appear to be two years older. I suppose that he figured that sooner or later we'd turn pro, and if it was to be sooner, he wanted us to be prepared for every possibility. But of course, he didn't tell us that. In those days, changing one's birth certificate was really not that uncommon, and a lot of guys who did made the change, was just to be able to join the military, which for a long time was a far more secure job than having to wait out the depression at home, on soup kitchen lines. I think we all sensed that war

41

was near, and that sooner or later, most of our fine young men would be drafted.

The Great Depression had continued in earnest in 1937, with Franklin Delano Roosevelt in his third term as President. But since FDR became President in 1928, the economy had improved quite a bit. And everyone knew that the time was coming, when a decision had to be made by our President to declare war or remain neutral. Congress also seemed to be divided on that issue. We hoped that we would continue to remain neutral, but deep inside, we all knew that Hitler's expansionist policies in Germany had to be stopped, and England and France couldn't do it without our help.

But at this time Adolph Hitler was still in the process of consolidating his power in Germany, and the anti-Jewish pogroms (exterminations) had begun. Hitler had also invaded and taken over Austria and Poland, which then caused Britain and France to declare war on them. Germany already had made alliances with other countries like Japan and Italy who would soon become our enemies also, and Der Fuhrer also put together a non-aggression pact with Josef Stalin in Russia, which Hitler would eventually violate, possibly becoming his biggest mistake of the war. The Nazi armies had previously taken control of Czechoslovakia. Uncle Johnny was very concerned, because in Europe, our families would be considered gypsies because of our heritage, and rumors were flying that the Nazis were enslaving and exterminating Jews and gypsies and homosexuals en masse, in the newly occupied lands.

"We have to stop that cold blooded stinking bastard now", Uncle Johnny would say. But America was not yet prepared for a long war, and our government seemed to be closing their eyes to the ever increasing atrocities that were being reported but not as yet been confirmed, at least to the average citizen. So, as far as anyone knew these rumors were just that or at the very least unproven, and besides, Europe was very far away, across the Atlantic Ocean. While Europe was at war, as it always seemed to be, America was still at peace.

Johnny wanted to enlist in the Army because he felt that it was just a matter of time till "FDR had the guts to take on that SOB Nazi bastard. All our President thinks of is getting us out of this God damn depression. He acts like we're not part of the real world. It looks like we'll have no depression and no country left by the time he's thrown out of office." He was correct, of course, at least according to much of the thinking in our neck of the woods, during that era. But Uncle Johnny was not eligible to enlist due to his black lung disease (and probably his age, as well, since he was in the mid 40's at the time). Besides this was before the "Uncle Sam Want's You" and "Rosie the Riveter" recruiting drives had begun.

And all the while America was continuing in the midst of the depression and Roosevelt seemed to be devoting all his time and energy to government projects to put as many Americans as possible back to work. The CCC

(Civilian Conservation Corps) and the TVA (Tennessee Valley Authority) for example may have employed a lot of Americans.

At the same time, Adolph Hitler, the mad man in Germany, was starting to move his armies all across Europe and perhaps eventually the world. Few people around us doubted his intentions.

Did work really matter? There was what seemed to be a great many German American people called 'brown shirts' who took the side of the Nazis We had more than our share in Philadelphia. There were also a lot of well-meaning Americans who felt that we should remain neutral and isolated and not worry about the growing takeover of the European Continent by what the papers were now calling the 'Third Reich'.

Mom would never mention Hitler or the Nazis but she was obviously concerned, reading the paper and listening to the news on our radio every evening after work and on Sunday, which was her day off. I still think, but never really found out for sure, that she had some relatives living in Hungary and Yugoslavia, who were either in constant danger or who had disappeared without a trace. It was a topic she never wanted to discuss.

But to Billy and I, the clouds of war seemed very far away, and we really didn't care or think much about it at the time. We figured it was just Europe's problem, certainly not ours. Sometimes we would both agree with Uncle Johnny's political views, just to keep him happy, but other than that, it was not a big concern to us. All we wanted to do was take care of ourselves by learning to box and of course, learn self-defense. The rest of the world may have been far away, but little did we know it was growing closer and closer to us with every passing day.

Billy and I had continued to work out regularly at the South St. Gym, three days a week, after school, and on both weekend days, at least during the hours that the gym was open. We weren't trying to build our body mass, since Paulie would always tell us that we could never be effective boxers if we were muscle-bound. Looking at the muscles on some of the fighters of today, I have to wonder if that was sound advice. It sure didn't hurt us though. "Speed was da real answer", "Speed and quick reflexes". Paulie would continually impress on our young minds, "and you had to learn that the 'sweet science' of boxing meant hitting and not getting hit in return. Ya gotta learn to slip der punches.

Occasionally Billy and I would spend some time tossing a heavy medicine ball back and forth. It was just something to keep us busy until Paulie would find the time to leave whichever fighter he happened to be working with at the time, and get around to us, to help continue with our training.

And on those five 'go to the gym days' we always had to run a mile, and more often than not, two, no matter how cold or wet the weather was. "Der running builds up stamina and gives ya character", Paulie would always say. Afterwards we headed directly to the gym where we had to do 100 or

45

more push-ups, 100 sit-ups, shadow box and jump rope before we would be able to hit the showers and end the day. The rest of the routine was usually the easy and fun part, sparring, sometimes in the ring, sometimes shadow boxing in front of a mirror and hitting the speed and the heavy bag until Paulie would yell "Time!" for us to stop. The routine, though exciting to us at first, was beginning to get a bit boring. The big benefit that we could immediately see is that we were able to get a very good nights sleep.

It was during this time that I noticed that another change had come over Billy. He had now became stubborn, arrogant and could even be very nasty at times, although rarely ever with me. He appeared to have developed a real mean streak, although he never told me why. When I asked he said I was wrong and that he didn't know what I was talking about.

Somehow Billy had gained more confidence than me, and had become determined that no one was going to ever push him around again. To the best of my knowledge, no one ever did. Maybe the attitude change came because although we had the same upbringing, we had different fathers or maybe just because he was smaller and felt the need to fight to survive.

Billy and I almost always sparred in the ring with each other, and outside the gym, we'd go behind the fence and workout together as well. There never seemed to be any other guys in the gym who were our age, or size, so it seemed to us that we were destined to always face-off against each other. Very soon that became routine and our moves predictable. I knew Billy's tactics like a book and he knew mine as well. He had much faster hand and foot speed than I did, while, perhaps because of my size and age, I was the harder hitter. But even that one advantage didn't last long.

Billy was a fast learner. Maybe he felt he needed that extra edge, and he learned how to turn over a punch much faster than I could, which gave him better power because he was landing flush with his knuckles. Paulie or one of the other veterans who hung out in the gym would supervise the sparring sessions, but as one would expect, even Paulie realized that there would come a time when we felt we could no longer learn anything new by fighting with each other.

When we told him that we felt we just weren't learning enough that Paulie put on the big mitt, and got in the ring with us, one at a time. Moving around from left to right, and then back and forth again, and yelling things like, "jab", "hook", "uppercut" "Turn it over". We chased him around the ring following his instructions, and hitting the oversized glove that resembled a catcher's mitt. "Again! Again!" he would yell out to us. We'd work up one heck of a sweat before we hit the showers.

Mom knew that we were going to the gym, but never asked what we did there. We were sure she knew. And while it was obvious that she didn't approve, she allowed us to 'learn about self defense' as long as we remained in school and kept our grades up. I think that Uncle Johnny had spoken to her about the importance of boxing, not only for our self-defense, but to help us learn discipline and gain confidence, so that we could take care of ourselves.

We were still getting robbed on a fairly regular basis, but that was because we seemed to always be outnumbered and never had the confidence (or stupidity) to fight back. But Billy and I both fully understood that the day would soon come when we would be able to retaliate and finally keep our money and regain our long-lost pride. That memorable day would come a lot sooner than either of us ever expected.

We had been working out at the gym regularly, for about six months, and I recall that it happened in the fall, because of the large pile of wet fallen leaves we had slipped on, when our first even-up confrontation occurred.

We were walking home together from school, during a light drizzle, when two guys in heavy, torn sweaters, one a lot bigger then either of us were, jumped out from behind a shrub, brandishing a pocket knife. They menacingly demanded all of our money. But it was a two on two confrontation and this was one that we were prepared for.

"Get lost! Who do we look like, your two-bit, poor excuses for parents? Let them support you. We don't give handouts to fucking bums like you!" Billy said, suddenly displaying a new-found confidence and it didn't take much to realize that my little brother had now become the brave one. I was fully prepared to just turn over the little bit of cash that we carried, because

it really wasn't worth fighting over. I guess that I felt that way pretty much from the force of habit than from fear. Obviously I was very surprised with Billy's demeanor.

"Hey, Punk, are you talking to us? The larger of the two said to Billy in a very confrontational manner. He was wearing an old blue flannel shirt under the sweater, and old, ripped, dirty looking torn blue jeans and some very badly worn out sneakers. Unexpectedly, Billy had forced the issue and I quickly realized that this was now the time for us to use the months of hard training that we had received in the gym or it would have all gone for naught.

"You heard my brother, get lost, scumbags! Get a fucking job!" I was surprised at the sound of my own voice now, and quickly peeled off my light jacket, still secretly wishing that these two guys would just turn tail and run.

Surprisingly, the smaller of the two thugs, who had brown eyes, freckles and blonde unruly hair and who looked somewhat younger than Billy and I, turned to walk away, but the bigger one grabbed him by the neck. "We ain't gonna let these two punks get away with that, are we Jackie? We came here to get their money and we ain't goin to leave without all of it. Besides, we ain't gonna let them insult our parents, are we?" Obviously it wasn't intended to be a question. The youth he called Jackie slowly turned and walked back to his friend's side. "No way, Tom", he responded, trying to be brave. "I was just getting myself ready to kick some ass!"

Billy and I planted our feet solidly, but stood on the balls of them, as we had been taught to do in the gym, and waited for the assault we knew would be quickly coming. Billy intentionally faced the bigger guy named Tom who held the knife, leaving me with a younger, smaller kid to dispose of.

Tom, the bigger kid stepped forward with a sneer on his face and wielding a rusty pocket knife in his hand outstretched. "Are you schmuck's deaf or just stupid? I ought to cut your tongues out! I said to give me all your money, now!"

Again it was Billy who took the initiative. He knocked Tommy's outstretched arm out of the way, the knife falling loudly to the concrete, leaped up and landed the sweetest right uppercut to his nose that I think I've ever seen, even till this day. It brought a stream of blood from his nostrils and tears to his eyes. The younger kid, named Jackie, just turned and quickly took off, making it two against one, but I knew Billy wouldn't want me to interfere. Suddenly Billy and I now had the advantage, which I believe was a first for us.

The bully lunged for his knife, which I easily stepped up and kicked far out of his reach. He took another step towards Billy, but it was my turn now, and the adrenaline was flowing and my heart was beating faster than I could ever remember. I could sense all the power and frustration that had built up inside me over the years of being taken advantage of. I pushed Billy aside, and landed three straight jabs to his already bloody face, followed by an uppercut that must have knocked out some of his teeth, because a flow of blood came pouring from his mouth.

The young thug wiped the blood, which was now flowing freely, on his sweater and shirtsleeve, and turned to leave. "You guys haven't seen the last of me. I'll get you next time and kick both of your fucking butts! You will wish that this day never happened."

"We'll look forward to it", Billy said bravely, staring him in the face, "Whenever you're ready, you big, fat, ugly jerk!"

Billy then turned to me. "Why did you do that, Tony? I wanted him for myself. Did you think I was afraid or couldn't handle him?"

"No, Billy", I lied. "His friend took off and I just wanted a piece of the action. Why should you have all the fun?"

I picked up the old, rusty pocketknife from the pile of leafs, folded it and put it in my jacket pocket as a handy reminder of our first victory, which although Billy didn't like it, was a team effort.

As Billy and I slowly walked home, we were almost hoping for another confrontation. I don't remember ever feeling that good. And Billy and I couldn't wait to get back to the gym the next day and tell Paulie what had happened. He taught us how to defend ourselves by boxing and we knew that he would be very proud of us.

"I'll betcha that Tom is one scumbag who will never bother us again," Billy said. "We showed him good, didn't we?"

"There were two guys," I corrected him. "You really think we're finished with them"? I asked.

Billy s just smiled and nodded.

Paulie, as expected, was very proud of us and told us so, in no uncertain terms. But he was not as proud as Uncle Johnny was. Johnny took us to the corner candy store and brought us both a big chocolate ice cream soda. "Great going, kids", he said. "You now have a new tool to use in your life, but use it wisely and never let it use you. Only fight when you have to, but when you do, fight to win! I wouldn't want you kids to become bullies like those guys you just fought." It sounded like pretty good advice to me, although Billy's attitude was constantly changing and I wasn't sure that we were still on the same page, but that also was going to change.

In retrospect, I think that better advice from Johnny would have been for us to pick our spots. Know when to fight and when to back down. That advice would have saved us a few stitches and teeth, as we would quickly learn.

Mom was very upset when she saw the streaked blood stains on our shirts, but was quickly relieved when she learned that none of the red splatter belonged to us. Still, she was the only one we told, that didn't really seemed pleased with what we had just done. "It's good that you two boys were able to defended yourselves", she said, "but I'd still prefer you just give them the money, rather than fight. Violence has never solved anything".

Unlike Johnny and Paulie, the guys in the gym didn't seem quite so excited about our first victory. It was almost like they had expected it. But then again, people don't always show their true feelings. "You boys have learned quickly," Paulie said. "Maybe it's time I started getting you some real fights, with a referee. I think it's time that you kids joined the ranks of the amateurs, and worked your way up, and you can make a few bucks in the process. You can use the money, right?" "Okay", we yelled loudly, together. We couldn't wait to have our first bout.

Billy and I felt like we could now conquer the entire world. It seemed like there was nothing in this that world we couldn't do. The confidence that we had gotten in just a few minutes, against two bullies, was going rapidly to our heads. We thought that we could and would fight anyone, anywhere and at anytime, and win. Of course we were wrong, there was always going to be someone better. So it was a false sense of confidence, and it soon became part of a tough but very important lesson for us to learn.

The next few weeks we were walking slowly home from school, far slower than we usually did, since we no longer had any fear of the street gangs, As we should have expected, we were soon surrounded by about five of these bullies. I quickly saw that one of them was Tommy, the big kid whom we had beaten up the last time he tried to rob us, although it was in self-defense. He had a bandage on the bridge of his nose and was still sporting two black eyes and a swollen lip. He needed a shave, but I'm sure he didn't care about that at the moment, and in truth, neither did we. He also had a very angry look on his face. But this time he held no weapon that Billy and I could see, which, considering the odds that were already against us, was a bit of a relief.

On one hand we were very pleased to see the damage we had done to him, but somehow, seeing how many thugs he had with him this time brought out some fear in us, or at least in myself, which I had thought was long gone. Billy tossed off his jacket and stood his ground as I quickly looked for a place for us to run. Seeing none, I followed Billy's lead and took off my jacket also, and then we braced ourselves for the battle that we knew was going to happen. We stood back to back to give ourselves a better chance. It was an unfair contest, akin to General Custer and the 7th Cavalry at the Little Big Horn. However, the good news was that Billy and I both survived. Although we knew that the cuts and bruises would upset mom and we thought maybe Uncle Johnny and Paulie would be ashamed of us.

"I told you I'd get even, punks," the big kid named Tommy said "and now your butts are mine!" It was hard to say who he was directly talking to, Billy or me, as we both had damaged him a bit. But it didn't really matter as all five of the gang seemed to converge on us at once, and quickly wrestled us to the ground, with the added help of the wet and slippery, newly fallen leafs. They pummeled and kicked us until they got tired. Being unable to use our hands and feet, we took the beating without a tear and they took our money and jackets and left.

"Bring more money with you the next time, punks!" Tommy said. Billy again surprised me, jumping up quickly, wiping the blood dripping from his nose, as I slowly got off the wet leafs, "You ain't got the guts to fight me even up. You need a gang around you! Hey, I'm a lot smaller than you! You're nothing but a damn, fat, ugly coward!"

The message, although accurate, left something to be desired, considering the circumstances, his timing seemed to be pretty bad. Because he knew that he had us hurt and outnumbered, Tommy said with a sneer on his lips, "How about right now, kid? You man enough?"

Billy assumed the correct boxing stance that he had learned in the gym and awaited the attack that was sure to come. I was amazed as Billy was a good five or six inches shorter and weighed far less than his adversary, not to mention that he was injured and bleeding from the nose and mouth. I just watched silently, intending to protect him in the event that the other gang members would jump in. I knew I couldn't do much against four bullies, but I had an obligation to protect my kid brother. And I wasn't going to let him down, no matter what.

Fortunately, for us I think, Tommy glanced at Billy, then back at me, and obviously decided that perhaps my kid brother was right. He shook his head and laughed with bravado, "I did enough damage to your sorry ass for one day. I have to leave you assholes in one piece so I can get more money from you again next week! Make sure you have it, and I want twice as much next time!" he boldly stated. He turned, spit, and walked away with his gang of five thugs behind him.

"You're not getting another cent from us, you fucking jack off, Billy yelled. I thought for a brief moment that despite the odds, Billy was going to take off after him, but although I'm sure that he did think about it, he wisely did not.

"Guess you were wrong about not seeing Tommy again," I said to him, checking my sore body for broken bones."

"Wrong? Tony, maybe I was wrong the last time but I will guarantee you that we'll never have to deal with him again. I swear to you he won't bother us ever again!"

I smiled. How could my little brother, Billy, who I used to always protect, think he could stop this big, ugly, arrogant bully who towered over him and outweighed him by what looked to me to be a good 50 pounds? I wondered where he had gotten all the confidence from.

The strange part is that Billy was right. We never did see Tommy again. I had assumed that he had moved away. As I now think back about it, with Billy, as hard-nosed as he had become, maybe he had sought Tommy out and taught him a lesson....or worse! But Billy was never to speak about it again, and I knew better than to ask.

Billy and I looked at each other, wiped ourselves off and again checked for any broken bones. Fortunately all that we could find was that we both had a little flow of blood from the few bruises and scrapes on our elbows and knees, and I had a cut on my upper lip and a bit of a headache. We both had a somewhat embarrassing wetness on the seat of our pants, from where we had gone down on the damp leaves, and hoped that those guys who had just attacked us didn't take notice and think we shit our pants.

But Billy and I knew that we were still in one piece and would be able to fight again.

Seeing there were no serious injuries, we decided to head directly to the gym to see if Paulie could give us some new ideas on defending ourselves when we were outnumbered.

"Well", Paulie said when he saw us, "what on earth happened to you two?"

We told Paulie what had happened and he listened quietly and intently. When we finished he just shook his head and said. "Okay, you guys seem to have had more than enough exercise for the day. No working out today. Go on home and come back here on Saturday. I can see that I have a few more things that I'm going to have to teach you. But, you'll learn, I guarantee that!"

He could see by our expressions that we were disappointed. We wanted to stay and to learn how to defend ourselves when we were out-numbered, and we wanted to learn right then and there. Sadly, Paulie had no direct answer for us, and left the solving of this situation to our own problem solving abilities, for the time being.

"Okay, I can't teach you guys how to fight when you're badly outnumbered, like today, but I can tell you that you should always go after the ringleader first. Usually if he's hurt, the rest of the guys will turn tail and run away. And Tony, I'm going to teach you how to create more damage to him by having you re-learn how to turn over a punch properly. You haven't been doing that lately". He bit down on his chewed up, unlit cigar.

I had a pretty good idea what Paulie was talking about, as we had learned how to turn over a punch from one of the other fighters in the gym, and it was something I didn't feel comfortable doing, I found that it really hurt my wrist. But Billy was able pick up the technique very quickly whereas I had not. We were also a little disheartened that Paulie had no other answer to our pressing question, what were we to do when we're outnumbered? Maybe there was no other answer. We decided to ask Uncle Johnny.

After dinner, we went over to his house, and Uncle Johnny was a bit more help. "Remember boys, I told you to always pick your spots, and to look for an opening, and this certainly wasn't one of those spots, as you had no openings. There are times you have to fight and there are times you have to run. But one thing I'll tell you, never, ever, get into a fight that you don't intend to win." He emphasized the words 'ever' and 'never!'

At this point in time we didn't fully understand his meaning. Why would anyone ever fight to lose? It was a bit confusing to us, but after talking it over between ourselves, the meaning of Uncle Johnny's words soon became crystal clear. Why take on a fight and risk getting hurt if you either don't intend to, or cannot win it? This was a lesson that was to prove invaluable in our later lives. Although Billy never again would show any fear of anyone. It was probably because he no longer feared anyone.

I could never figure Billy out. He was almost two full years younger than me, much smarter in school, an A student, and certainly not afraid of challenging anyone. I was older and bigger, but he was always much tougher, at least he seemed to be. To this day I still wonder what had made him that way.

Mom, Billy and I spent most of the holidays with Uncle Johnny, who always had plenty of room at his house, and always had a Christmas tree, with presents for all of us underneath. This year he had the same presents for Billy and me, a brand new pair of boxing gloves and leather head-gear to replace the ones we were using which by now were very badly worn.

We also spent New Years Eve at Johnny's house, listening to the radio and the crowds at Times Square in New York City, welcoming in the New Year by watching the ball fall from the tower, to the sound of great big band music.

In early 1940, Paulie had booked us for our first amateur bouts. We were used to the headgear because we sparred with it on in the gym, and the new ones that Uncle Johnny brought us, fit even better, as the old ones would sometimes slide over our eyes and block our vision..

But in the amateurs you didn't look for the knockout, you would win your fights mainly on points scored by punches landed in the appropriate area. And in truth, the old headgear, at least those that we wore before Johnny brought us the new ones for Christmas, kept sliding on our heads, and sometimes blocking our vision. We really didn't like wearing it, but that was required. So the head gear, which was adjustable, really came in handy

We breezed through our early amateur bouts with ease, probably because of the experience we had picked up on the mean streets as well as in the gym. We both won our first six amateur fights by knockout, which Paulie said was very hard to do, considering our opponents also had to wear head gear, which protected them for the most part, of a one punch kayo, and certainly cuts around the eyes. And these fights earned us a few bucks for our efforts which mom certainly appreciated when we turned the purses over to her.

Paulie was already talking to some of his friends and others about turning us pro early and training and managing us. He had already shown me how to correctly turn over a punch, so that the power of our knuckles would land with full force, and cause a lot more damage, something that Billy had obviously learned from the start.

In those days, almost no one would ask for a birth certificate, so although the law said you couldn't fight pro until you reached age 16. There were always ways of getting around it, including forging a birth certificate if needed, which we had just in the rare case that someone asked. A lot of kids who looked older than us were enlisting in the service.

Billy was tempted to get a copy of the forged record of his birth from Paulie, not for boxing, but instead to enlist in the Army. Like most Americans, he felt that sooner or later we would have to face the ever-growing threat of the Nazis and wanted to be prepared to serve our country. But you could see by his baby face features that he looked far too young and the birth certificate would probably be questioned by the military recruiter. But Billy tried anyway, and he even asked Paulie for the copy of the forged one that he had gotten for him illegally, but Paulie, not wanting to chance getting into trouble, or perhaps losing a great pro prospect to Uncle Sam, turned him down.

So here I was, 17 years of age, but pretty big considering, and able to get my first shot at the pros, if I wanted it, and I did, badly. Billy, who probably would have become a better pro fighter, looked way too young and small, and couldn't be seriously considered. A baby face may have been a plus for him with the ladies, but it certainly didn't help him as he was anxiously wanting to make a big name in a new career.

I couldn't decide what the right thing to do was. I knew that I could make some decent money fighting in 'smokers,' club fights which might have allowed my mom to stop working, or I could continue training, going to school and fighting as an amateur. It wasn't an easy choice because financially, times were still very hard. Paulie told me to do what I felt was right, because unlike my younger brother, I could get away with it. But I had promised mom that I would stay in school and get my diploma. The okay to turn pro that I needed, was really from Uncle Johnny, who had seen all of my amateur fights, and was always encouraging me. He didn't this time, however.

Johnny shook his head when I told him what Paulie wanted me to do. "Forget about it, Tony. You're not ready to fight pro yet and right now we don't need the money that badly that you should have to drop out of school. And you would certainly have to do that, to devote all the time that you need to train properly for the big boys. Keep on training and fighting with the kids your own age and weight. In a few years you'll be ready to be a solid pro. Who knows, maybe you can become another great fighter like Billy Conn, Harry Greb, Charley Burley, Ray Robinson, Archie Moore or Billy Soose".

"Maybe better", I added in a brief moment of wishful thinking.

I took Johnny's advice, because he seemed to know boxing almost as well as Paulie did, or at least we thought he did. I continued winning all my amateur fights, but now they seemed to be almost always by decision. I didn't know if I had lost my knockout punch or not. Billy was far more impressive and was tearing up the amateur lightweight kids, to the point where he was kayoing almost everyone, and no one wanted to fight him. He was even having a tough time getting any sparring in, except with me of course.

The street gangs? They were still out there, I guess they always were and always will be. But at this point in time, the older gang members were largely moving out into the slowly growing work force or hanging out on street corners or malt shops with their girlfriends, and they seemed to have far better things to do with their free time than rob innocent people.

The thought has remained in my mind for all these years that much of our safety may have been because of our amateur fights and our growing reputation as tough guys, that these thugs left us alone. But I guess I'll never really know the real reasons for sure.

The younger kids continued to form new gangs or took over the lead of old ones, but by now Billy and I had grown way too big for them to mess around with. And with learning self-defense from boxing, it would have been a big mistake on their part if they had.

But the focus of most of the people at that time was the war clouds that were rapidly forming over Europe and the rest of the free world. It soon became the major conversation point at our dinner table as well as in the gym. The key question was 'should we or shouldn't we send troops to help our allies in Britain.' Paulie, a veteran of WWI was gung ho and wanted us to get involved as soon as possible. But many others were just not sure what the right approach was.

We had been sending supplies to the British via the lend – lease program for some time, and had lost quite a few ships to enemy submarines, but to the best of anyone's knowledge, we weren't sending our boys….at least not yet.

Chapter III

'December 7, 1941, a day that will live in infamy'. These were just some of the words uttered of President Franklin Delano Roosevelt, now in his fourth and final term, which he would not live to complete. This was the day that the Nation of Japan launched a surprise attack on the American Naval Base at Pearl Harbor, Hawaii, killing thousands of our soldiers and sailors and wiping out almost our entire Pacific Fleet of 18 warships and 188 airplanes. This event united this country like never before in my lifetime, with the possible exception of September 11, 2001, with the cowardly World Trade Center attack in NYC, which probably did an even better job in uniting this great land.

Americans were horrified. We had become complacent for so long and the war that had been raging in the Pacific and Europe seemed so far away that we felt that it could never effect our lives.

How did we allow this tragedy to happen? What happened to our intelligence agencies? In Pearl Harbor, where we asleep at the wheel? There were reports that we had spotted the Japanese fleet and we should have expected the attack. To this day, no one seems to know for sure, or if they do, they aren't talking about it.

Rusty Rubin

So on that Sunday morning of December 7, 1941, this was truly the "United" States of America. After the sneak attack, many folks on the West Coast were expecting the Japanese invasion force to hit our shores at any time. We didn't know they had done their evil deed for the day and were returning home, victorious at least for the time being.

I remember many Americans even picking up rifles intending to defend the California Coastline in the event of an attack. Japanese Americans had begun to be rounded up and put into detention camps, imprisoned only because of their ancestry. That round-up was ultimately to be to our great shame instead of our safety, but we didn't know how to react at the time, and panic took control over logic.

And like September 11, 2001, everyone who was alive at the time can still remember where they were on that infamous day, when they first heard the horrific news. On Sept. 11, I was eating breakfast with the family in Florida, when the phone rang and my son told me to turn on the TV, that terrorists had flown a plane into the World Trade Center in NY. I switched on the boob tube and saw the second plane hit. We were all horrified.

World War II had begun in earnest for us and armament inflation, came about as a result of the wartime economy and helped put a lot of unemployed people to work in defense plants and other venues, as well as the military, so in effect, the great depression was now unofficially over.

As I recall, this was also the year that Germany broke their non-aggression pact with the Soviet Union and launched a surprise attack on their former ally. A mistake that may have cost them any chance they had of winning the war.

And I believe that it was also the first year for US Savings Bonds and food and gas Rationing Stamps were in usage. And in sports, New York Yankee center fielder Joe DiMaggio hit in 56 consecutive baseball games, a record that may never be broken. But more to the point, this event was something that happened at just the right time, to help us take our mind off the faraway conflict that had suddenly come to our shores and into all our lives.

Mom, Billy and I had just come home from church and were eating a late breakfast that quiet Sunday morning when the news came over the radio and mom, who was the only one listening just yelled out "Oh my God! We're being invaded!" I'll never forget those words. Although they were not true, they were just scary enough for us to believe at the time. She quickly got on the phone and called Uncle Johnny, who had already heard the shocking news report. He calmly told mom "Don't worry, we're not being invaded. We'll kick their asses and this war will be over in no time."

So suddenly America was truly the "United" States. Nothing divided us now. We were all as one. Gangs? Well even the mobsters wanted to join in the fight against the Japanese as well as their axis pals, Germany and Italy, and as it turns out, many actually did.

69

It didn't take long for President Roosevelt to ask Congress for a state of war to be declared between the United States and the Imperial Nation of Japan. And Congress quickly approved it. Russia, who had a non-aggression pact with the Nazis, didn't enter the war with the Allies at that time, but did later in the year when Germany surprised them and shocked the world by invading them. That in itself may have cost the Germans the war, it certainly played a major factor. They weren't equipped for the tough Russian winter and to have to fight on two fronts proved impossible. So Russia was first spared from an allied attack due to their proclaimed neutrality, and then the Nazis surprised them and the rest of the world by invading them. Adolph Hitler was a madman and certainly not a military genius.

Later on, after the German invasion was stopped at the gates of Stalingrad, the Russians would unite with the Allied forces to help destroy the German war machine by attacking them from the East. Of course America would continue to help them out as well with the Lend - Lease program. As I recall one of our key points of delivery to the Soviets was a seaport City named Minsk.

After America had declared war on Japan, Germany and Italy quickly followed by declaring war on Britain, France and America, and of course America immediately declared war on them, and the 'Big Clambake' that was to be World War II, was underway.

In what turned out to be a major mistake on our part, many proud Japanese Americans were rounded up and put in detention camps in California and I believe other West Coast States, as many Americans had become paranoid about those who looked different than we did and feared a plot from within. It was wrong and it was a very shameful part of our history, but, like slavery, it's also a historical fact and nothing can be done to change it or make it right.

The government also approved the rationing of gasoline, food and other necessities, and issued stamps to allow people to buy only what was thought to be their fair share of necessities that would not take from the war effort. Of course that created a booming black market for most of these items, if one wanted or needed more of those commodities and had the money to pay for it, and some actually did. Greed won out over caring and common sense, but fortunately not in very many instances, and the few that were caught were severely punished.

All though, we had already been involved in the war, through our Lend - Lease program, few were aware of the fact that we were sending arms and munitions to our allies to help them defend themselves against the relentless Nazi war machine. Their submarines seemed to be all over the Atlantic Ocean. We lost many ships and Merchant Marine sailors in the process. Still, sending our valiant young men to actually fight in battle after battle was quite a bit different.

Despite all the flag waving and patriotism, there still remained a small but very vocal group, mostly made up of German - Americans who wanted us to maintain our isolationist policies, even after the deadly attack on Pearl Harbor. They tried to keep us out of the war, but were badly outnumbered. These folks were far from honorable Americans in our eyes. But in this great land, all opinions are allowed and fortunately for us and the world they were a vocal but small group.

The Petrovic's were brought up to love and be very proud of our great Country, and Billy, although only fourteen then, wanted to join the Army. I guess it was his way of dealing with his frustrations and letting out his anger. I was 16, and I could have given the enlistment route a shot, because I was pretty big for my age. I decided against it. It wasn't that I was afraid to do my duty, I wanted to do my part, but because mom, who had been having health problems, needed me at home to take care of Billy. And so, at least for the time being I was going to remain home, continue to train, box and go to school. And all I could do for our brave boys overseas was say prayers for them in church, every Sunday.

I had about six or seven club fights, called 'smokers' for obvious reasons, which I was told is how all the youngsters started out in those days. I won all but one, which was scored as a 'no decision'. And I had suddenly found my KO punch again with five KO's in those six wins, and I had become what Paulie called a 'crowd pleaser'. I guessed it was because many times, after my fight, coins and bills (mostly coins) were tossed into the ring for me and my opponents, to split between us. It was a way to make us feel appreciated, and the extra money certainly didn't hurt our feelings. Some nights I'd make an extra $5 or $10 extra, and it would always come in handy.

Billy still had very few of these amateur fights, and won them all by knockouts. His frustration was becoming more and more obvious. Sometimes, he would come home from school in a very surly mood, throw his books on the bed, and slam his fist loudly against the wall. He wanted to fight. He needed to fight. That seemed to be the only outlet for his frustrations, and no one would take him on. His only pro ring experience came from working the spit bucket and mouthpiece in my corner during those smokers (fights held in small venues, in smoke filled rooms, hence the name).

While Billy seemed very excited and happy for me, doing so well in my fights, he always seemed to be carrying that huge chip on his shoulder. He clearly seemed to believe that of the two of us, he was the better puncher and boxer, and no one wanted to give him a chance to prove it in the ring. I hate to admit it, and certainly wouldn't at that time, but I would not have wanted to take him on in a serious fight. I still think that although he was a far bigger puncher than me, I could hit and run and out-box him all day. But I'm glad it had never come down to that.

Even mom, who although ill, still continued to work, and wasn't with us that often, could sense the dramatic change in Billy. But I was the one bringing home a few extra bucks now from the money thrown into the ring

73

by the crowd, during the smokers and along with my purses, our family lifestyle was improving greatly. Sadly Billy's moods and mom's health didn't improve.

Even Uncle Johnny sensed the severe change in Billy's attitude. He would call me aside and ask me what was wrong with my younger brother. I told him the truth, that I honestly didn't know. Although I thought it might be that he had built up all this rage inside himself and that he had little way of getting rid of it, except by doing roadwork, working out in the gym or fighting in the ring. And although not a bully by any stretch of the imagination, he loved to hurt people, but only in a fair fight.

In the gym, he was constantly pounding away at the heavy bag like he wanted to knock the stuffing out of it. I suppose that if it wasn't for boxing, Billy may well have also become like one of those street thugs, and would have ended up in jail or worse. In all honesty, at that moment in time, I wasn't completely sure that he hadn't become a bad apple. Our communication during this period was very bad. Few words were being exchanged between us. He ignored me as often as not, or answered with only 'yes' or 'no' or 'I don't care,' when possible.

Another good outlet for Billy's frustration was helping me train, running the mile or more beside me daily, and doing the same amount of push-ups which was also a source of relief, an outlet, for my kid brother. But I think the heavy bag had become both his best friend and worst enemy at that

74

time. He would always tear into it with a hatred he rarely showed elsewhere. There was little question in my mind that someday he would wind up killing an opponent in the ring, or even killing someone he didn't like, out of it.

I also recall once having asked Billy what was wrong, and all he said was "Wrong? Johnny, Can't you tell? How the hell can I ever become a fighter if no one has the balls to fight me? Everybody's scared of me. Even the Army doesn't want me. I feel like I'm just wasting my fucking time in this world! And you ask what's wrong? You're not blind!" It was a legitimate question, to which I didn't have any answer, except to point out that he was still too young for both turning pro and also for joining up and fighting for Uncle Sam.

My eighth pro fight took place in that year, and it was to be a fight to remember. I had just fought to a hard eight round decision win two weeks earlier, and I was a bit exhausted. I had never really wanted to fight more than once a month, but our family needed the money and I wasn't going to turn down anybody at anytime just because I didn't have the drive to fight more often.

This time I was going in against a tough fighter from the North side of Philadelphia. One who nobody else seemingly wanted to fight, named Bob Harrison, 12-0, a tall, sleek middleweight who was also on his way up the boxing ladder and was feared by most other young fighters as all his wins were by knockout. I wanted his head on my shield so I could move my pro

75

career along more quickly. This was going to be a very important fight for me.

I was advised by a lot of folks not to take the fight. Even if I would beat Harrison, he'd make me look bad in doing so. But how would I ever learn enough if I didn't meet all styles of opposition? This was going to be my first big money fight, since it was being held in the South Side movie theater, which held a heck of a lot more people than I had ever fought in front of before. I was guaranteed $50 if I won and $25 even if I lost, so it was by far going to be my biggest payday to date. That was a lot of money in those days, and this fight with Harrison was also going to be my first main event.

Paulie was still my manager and trainer and he had very specific instructions on how to both punch and defend myself against this soon-to-be arch rival. Paulie also had tried hard to discourage me from taking this fight because no one would throw any money into the ring, as Harrison was 'a plodding type of opponent, and would bore the crowd to sleep. He just won flat-out ugly.'

"That Bobby Harrison is a real dirty fighter," he told me. "He'll wait till the ref's vision is being blocked and then hit you with his head, his elbows or below the belt, whatever he can get away with. You'll be pissing blood for a week or more after the fight. He does whatever the fuck it takes to win, and he always finds a way. Once he softens you up, he uses a powerful right hook to the liver to get you to drop your guard and then throws his overhand right for his knockout punch. You have to use all your ring skills and work his body all the time. If he fouls you, do it back to him, but make sure the ref's not looking when you do. And for God's sake, Tony, if you get hurt, lean into him and tie him up."

"You have to *really* work the body, softening him up before looking for the KO. He's the first black guy you've fought, but don't let that change anything. He feels pain, cuts and bleeds red like everyone else. He'll pretend he's your friend in the ring, getting you to relax and make a mistake, and that's when he nails you. Don't expect an easy fight. Don't get cocky! Harrison is tough and this is not going to be a walk in the park for you, Tony."

A walk in the park? Obviously I had already known that, and I was also a bit surprised because there was never any talk of prejudice in my household or even in my neighborhood, as I recall. To our folks and our friends and neighbors, all people were the same. Didn't our Declaration of Independence proclaim that "All men are created equal? I never did understand racial hatred. Still can't till this day."

But this upcoming bout really didn't sound like it would be very much fun to me. All my previous fights had been relatively easy and lasted less than 10 rounds. This fight with Harrison was slated to be my first 10-rounder.

Still, I was excited and confident, and certainly not afraid to take on anyone. Since the fight would be held at the local theater, I felt sure the crowd would be on my side. But even that knowledge did not take away the butterflies that I was feeling in the pit of my stomach. I had never been badly hurt in the ring before, and I didn't want to start now. I had never really felt this uptight before a bout before, maybe because I had never experienced a very tough match before, and Paulie had never been so serious in giving me advice. He was clearly worried, so was I.

Still, hindsight is always 20-20. Looking back, I should have paid much more attention to Paulie's specific instructions, which would have saved me from the unanticipated end result. Despite Paulie's constant warnings, I just wasn't prepared for what was about to happen. In truth, even if I would have remembered all the instructions, I doubt it would have changed the outcome of the fight in any way.

Paulie, with Billy alongside, holding the rusty spit bucket, and I, walked down the densely smoke filled aisle, noticing the circle of pale gray smoke that surrounded the ring, and seemed to be floating onto the stage where the ring was set up. I noticed that almost every guy in the packed house seemed to be wearing a brimmed fedora hat. But once I reached the ring, I was concentrating only on the fight and not on the cheering crowd.

Paulie slid underneath the top ring rope first, carrying my stool, and placing it in my corner by the ring-post. Billy followed him in, putting the spit bucket and mouthpiece, on the side of the wooden stairs that led up to the ring apron. He then climbed into the ring, holding the top strand high with his hand and using his foot to lower the middle strand of rope so I could climb onto the badly worn, blood stained ring apron. The crowd roared loudly as I entered the ring, my gloves held high in appreciation of the applause.

In those days, there were only three strands of rope surrounding the ring. Today, they use four, and I have to believe that is one very smart move that has allowed many fighters to continue their career. The fourth strand of rope protects fighters from hitting the ring edge hard when going down, and ultimately it does save lives.

I heard what I thought to be a lot less cheering when Bob Harrison ducked under the top strand of rope and entered the ring, also holding his hands high, waving to the crowd. Actually, if I recall correctly there were almost as many boos for my opponent as there were cheers for me, and I didn't know if it was because he was thought of as a dirty fighter or because I was the local favorite in this bout. Probably it was as much a combination of both.

The referee called us to the center of the dimly lit ring. I wore black trunks and a pair of black, slightly worn blue gloves, and high-top white sneakers. Harrison, who was to be my first, but certainly not my last minority opponent, was wearing red and white trunks and black tennis shoes with white laces and red gloves.

As we were being introduced to the crowd by the ring announcer, I also noticed that there were some local press on hand and a microphone in the first row told me that a radio station was airing this bout. Wow, my name on the radio. To me it seemed as if this was this were my first world title fight. It didn't help the butterflies though. In fact it made them flutter some more.

Bob Harrison was a tall, lean but heavily muscled, good looking black guy, who seemed to exude a lot of self confidence. We looked each other in the eye as the referee barked out his instructions. I never gave any thought to the instructions, I doubt any fighter listens because he's heard them many times before and is too busy staring down his opponent. I had heard the same words on many previous occasions, and the key words for this fight was going to be, "protect yourself at all times."

We touched gloves and went back to our corners, and I saw Harrison kneel and cross himself, asking for God's blessing. I laughed to myself, fully believing he needed a lot more than his religion to beat me. Talk about false confidence. Although I did think about doing the same thing, just to show him that the Lord doesn't play favorites.

But I didn't bother to go through the same ritual, having been taught at home and at church that the Lord treats everyone the same.

The loud clang of the opening bell sent us to center ring, and as I reached out my gloves in a gesture of sportsmanship to Harrison, he quickly brushed them aside and went on the offensive at once. I was caught by surprise. I didn't know it was coming, but in retrospect, I should have, and suddenly I was backed up against the ropes, with Harrison banging away at my face and body. I covered up, and heard Billy yelling, to me, "clinch Tony, clinch".

Clinch. I never had to hold on before. And Billy was certainly not standing in my corner, where he was supposed to stay, and as I was told later, he was told to try to follow me around the ring and relay to me the instructions, given to him by Paulie.

But, following instructions, I grabbed Harrison's left arm, trying to hold it close to my body, and I gave him a big bear hug to prevent him landing anything solid. As he worked hard to push me away. I heard the referee yell 'break', and as I quickly opened up my hands to comply, Harrison, instead of breaking, took a step back and landed a huge right hand that sent me sprawling, face first, to the canvas. I remember the referee was counting over me and the crowd booing loudly as I tried to rise. But my legs refused to answer the instructions that were being sent to them from my brain, and I was counted out. For a couple of hours in the dressing room, I felt for the first time what a hangover felt like.

Billy was livid to say the least, at both Harrison for hitting on the break and the referee for not disqualifying him. He jumped into the ring to first see if I was okay, and seeing that I was then went charging after Harrison who was having his gloves taken off in his corner. Billy pushed his way through his corner men, grabbed him, and turned him around and landed a perfectly thrown left hand, that knocked Harrison to his knees. When the referee and Harrison's corner tried to pull Billy off, he instinctively turned quickly towards them and another left knocked the referee flat on the canvas. Billy was cursing him loudly as well, but fortunately he had caused no permanent damage to anyone.

Billy, Paulie and I both felt that Harrison should have been disqualified for hitting on the break, but the referee had told us before the fight to protect ourselves at all times, and I certainly didn't. Sure it was an illegal move on Harrison's part, but should have been expected by me, and he got away with it, and in so doing, had put the first loss on my previously unblemished record.

Sad to say that a wild riot then ensued in the arena. Chairs, beer bottles, and other items were thrown into the ring and the chairs were also used by the fans on the folks who were unfortunate enough to be sitting next to them and rooting for someone other than whom they did. Both Harrison and the ref were injured in the fracas. The police were quickly called in and when it was over, Billy was behind bars, along with a lot of fans that had taken various sides for this fortunately very abbreviated riot. .

In truth, the riot lasted much longer than my battle with Harrison, which was halted at 1:44 of the opening round. I guess it was really Billy who gave the crowd their money's worth and the police all they could handle trying to control him, and then some.

The story of the fight/riot was well covered by the press. The story and photos were all over the front page of the newspaper. It was the lead story on the local news on the radio as well. To say that mom was not upset by the adverse publicity would be like saying it snows in the middle of the summer. She was livid, mainly at Billy, that someone in her family could cause so much trouble. For awhile, I really thought she'd never allow me to fight again. But I was wrong. Maybe it was the money involved that was going to improve our fortune in life, or maybe she felt that fighting in the ring was better than fighting in the streets. She was getting pretty high medical bills, so her decision was probably a combination of many factors. I believe that Billy was her favorite and mom clearly didn't want to punish him.

The fight itself lasted all of 104 seconds, and other than a bad headache, a cut and swollen lip, I came out of it just fine, except of course, for the loss. Harrison showed no visible damage from me, but had a cut on his forehead from being hit with a beer bottle. Why should he have had any damage from me, anyway? I don't think I ever laid a glove on him. I honestly feel that the referee, who was hit in the head with a chair and was hospitalized, got the worst of it, and somehow, I really didn't mind that much, since it was quite obvious to me as well as the local media, which combatant he had favored.

We didn't get a dime from our purses for that fight right away, but what we did get was a rematch, with a different referee and at a much bigger venue, with the purses almost doubled. So instead of coming out on the short end of the stick, it worked out well, long term for all of us.

After a long night in jail, along with much of the crowd in the packed drunk tank, Uncle Johnny, who told Billy how proud he was of him for standing up for me, bailed him out. And as a result of him showing a display of awesome power in the ring, Billy was to be on the undercard of our rematch, having his first pro bout, as a lightweight. He was going to be matched against one of Harrison's corner guys, the one who was trying to break up the fight and who happened to be hit and floored by Billy in the melee that night. The purse for the winner of Billy's fight was $10 and the loser got $5. But Billy, who was only 14, was never really interested in the money, he just badly needed that outlet for his frustrations. He finally found a way to achieve that, although it was far from planned that way. And it was a very costly intervention, since he had to repay Uncle Johnny the bail money percentage that he had put up.

Actually, Billy didn't have to repay him, as Johnny told him that he did the right thing and was very proud of him. Billy was brought up like I was, never to owe anyone, anything, even family. So the debt was repaid in full after Billy's fight.

At the time, boxing in the 'City of Brotherly Love' was a bit on the ropes itself. No one really wanted to risk having the sport suspended in Philadelphia as it had been in a few other locales. I learned that some people had to be paid off under the table, and all the charges against Billy, except the fine, was dropped. But the fans and the press would remember Billy's unpredictable actions a lot longer than the legal system would.

One of the main conditions for the rematch was a different referee for both bouts, which all parties agreed upon. This time a much larger police presence was to be on hand to try and prevent another riot. They also wanted me to replace Billy in my corner, since he was going to be fighting that night also, but this we refused and the promoters eventually relented.

Paulie had taken over Billy's career at once, and was working hard training him as well as myself. And, suddenly sparring partners for Billy were readily found, but because of his punching power, still very hard to keep. But, they were suddenly available, maybe because Paulie figured he would now be able to afford to pay for them.

So, although I was very disappointed in suffering my first professional loss, things were now looking up for both the 'Fighting Petrovic Brothers' as we had now become known.

The rematch was held about six weeks later, in a newly built arena on the North side, so the fans on hand were far more numerous, and in favor of

Harrison and his cornerman, who was fighting Billy in the semi-main. The referee was also from Harrison's side of the tracks. In short, it looked like the deck was really stacked against us, even more so this time. But we demanded the rematch and in order to get it, we had to agree to their terms. After all Harrison did beat me.

Before the fights, Paulie had a suggestion for us, which he made in the small dressing room. "This is Harrison's area. You kids have absolutely no chance of getting a decision here. Every close round will be scored against you. You'd better be able to turn over all your punches because you both are going to need a knockout to win. Look for the opening and land that big punch. Don't forget to turn it over! You've got the power, use it! Don't fuck around and try to box with these guys. You won't win a round on the scorecards anyway". I believe the suggestion was meant more for me than for Billy, who seemed to have unbelievable power for a kid his size.

Then Paulie turned and looked me right in the eye. "Tony, you should have learned a very valuable lesson in your last fight. Don't make the same mistake again! You get hurt you clinch and don't break until he does first. And if he fights dirty, you wait till you have the referee out of position and then you fight dirty also. It's got to be an eye for an eye."

I just looked at Paulie and nodded. This time I understood very well.

This was a much bigger arena, obviously made in the last few years for both boxing and wrestling. The crowd was exceptionally loud and obviously on Harrison's side. But we also knew that Uncle Johnny would be sitting at ringside and rooting for us. The microphone was hung on a long cord on the light fixture above the ring, where it could be raised or lowered for the use of the ring announcer.

Billy had the first match, against an older, much taller guy, who obviously had a lot of experience. You could tell by his paunch that he had a weight advantage or maybe it would be a disadvantage, as he was obviously way out of shape. But Billy didn't need to worry about that.

We were all more concerned about the seemingly hostile crowd who obviously didn't like Billy's actions in his previous ring experience against his opponent, who was much older than he was, and wanted revenge.

But, after two rounds of feeling each other out and looking for weaknesses, Billy saw his opening. Judging by his large gut, obviously he hadn't fought or trained hard in a while, he dropped the left hand that was guarding his left temple. That was all opportunity that Billy needed and like a cat he pounced, landing a huge overhand right, flush, right on target. The guys knees buckled and another quick right hand to the jaw provided the finishing touch. Billy's fight ended that suddenly, less than a minute into round three. The crowd booed, but in all honesty couldn't have been that surprised by the outcome.

Both Paulie and Uncle Johnny and I were on our feet cheering for Billy, who appeared to have everything it took to become a world champion. But the crowd was booing my brother loudly as Billy's hand was raised in triumph. A few tomatoes and other fruits were thrown at Billy, standing at center ring with his hands raised. I was a bit surprised that he didn't pick one up and throw it back, but he surprisingly remained in control of his temper. I was the one who thought about finding out who was flinging the fruit at him, but I was up next, so I quickly let the thought pass.

Suddenly I noticed a familiar female figure sitting next to Uncle Johnny, cheering for Billy. At first I thought it was Aunt Jen, but it was mom. To this day I have no idea how Johnny had managed to talk her into coming to the fight. But obviously it gave Billy, who had seen her while he was getting his instructions from the referee, and now myself, that extra incentive to impress her with our ability and skills. Billy had done his job and done it well, and soon I would have my chance. It was the first and the only one of our fights that mom was to attend.

Two fights later (unknown till the last minute to me, they changed Billy's from the semi-main into a 4-rounder) and it was my turn to walk down the aisle to the ring. Instead of the normal nervous butterflies in my gut, I was very angry and eager to avenge my only loss. Unlike Billy's opponent, I knew that Harrison, was in better shape and with more recent experience, would look for an opening and try to do something illegal, while the ref was out of position and unable to see it. I had no desire to taste this guy's surprising power any longer than I had to. But I was also prepared to use dirty tactics in return, if the occasion demanded it.

We met in the center of the ring, with the new, younger black referee giving instructions. He seemed to know Harrison's reputation as he was looking at him as he showed us what he would or would not allow. And staring directly and pointing a finger at Harrison said "No hitting on the break this time or I'll disqualify you." Harrison nodded. He really didn't seem like a bad guy; just a fighter doing what he had to do in order to earn a living and support his family.

Not that it really mattered to me, because I was determined to end this fight before he had a chance to try anything illegal to slow me down. My mind was made up. This was going to be my fight!

The bell rang and this time it was Harrison's turn to stick out his gloves in a gesture of good luck. While I didn't want to have to resort to his dirty tactics, I stepped back. "Not this time", I said. Harrison withdrew his extended glove and shrugged. The crowd booed my obvious poor showing of sportsmanship. "Sorry about last time," Harrison told me. But I didn't believe him for a minute. The crowd booed loudly when I went back to my corner. I heard the loud boos directed at me, but I didn't care. My focus this night was on beating Harrison, and nothing else.

Harrison was pretty fast, and as I approached him, he started to take the offensive, jabbing and cutting off the ring, and looking for an opening. Something I was determined not to give him.

"Jab, jab, jab" I heard Paulie yell. Since I had a longer reach, the advice made sense, and I fired off three consecutive left jabs to his face, looking for an opening. The last two of my hooks were blocked. "Turn it over, Tony! Turn over the fucking jab!" Paulie yelled.

My jab, which I didn't feel was my Sunday punch (or any other day for that matter) seemed to be an annoyance at best for Harrison. Who took a step back and threw a jab of his own, which I easily picked off with my left forearm.

It was pretty much that way throughout most of the first round, but the rounds that followed were quite another matter.

Paulie knelt beside me, as I sat on my stool between rounds. He told Billy to put some ice water on my head, and I also drank a bit, spitting the rest out into the spit bucket. "Good round, Tony", he said. "Now what I want you to do is get out there and work da body. He's got a little bit of a gut on him, and sooner or later his arms will tire and his guard is going to come down. When it does, you land that big right hand. But don't let him get ya on the ropes again. He knows that's where you're most vulnerable. Do you understand me?"

I nodded, by now I had learned to listen to Paulie's instructions, but although he was giving me sound advice, I pretty much knew what had to be done to win this fight, or at least I thought that I did.

It seems like Harrison had gotten similar advice from his corner, because he came out throwing his left jab to my body and eagerly looking for the opening that I had no intention of giving him. The difference was that he was looking for that one solid knockout punch, while I was working the body, trying to bring his hands down and open him up for my Sunday punch, although I'm not completely sure if I even had one at that time.

But rounds two through six followed the same pattern. Every time Harrison tried to land low blows when the ref wasn't looking, I did the same thing. Seems like since neither of us got caught or did any damage to the other, as the ref was either inexperienced or constantly out of position and didn't see, or maybe he just didn't care. He obviously wanted a more definitive outcome to this bout than our previous one, which he obviously was familiar with.

In round seven, Harrison came out, deciding to surprise me by fighting out of a crouch. I wasn't familiar with this style of boxing, so I continued using my jab, but I was having a hard time landing solid shots to his body, because it was covered, with him using this new stance. I was trying to hear Paulie and Billy yelling from the corner, they were yelling, "Uppercut, uppercut", but the noise of the crowd made it impossible for me to hear. For the first time in my ring career I was somewhat lost in the ring. I tried to muscle Harrison closer to my corner so I would be able to hear the instructions, but he was far too experienced to allow that to happen.

I finally got in close and landed a few solid blows, but then Harrison suddenly straightened up, his head landing sharply above my right eye. Blood started flowing down my cheek and the crowd started cheering on their local hero, loudly. I don't know if the ref saw what I thought was a deliberate head butt or not, but he didn't warn Harrison about it, although I complained and Paulie and Billy were also yelling some choice words at the ref, from the corner.

The blood quickly mixed with my sweat and was now running into my eyes, and I knew I had to do something or the fight could have been stopped, and not in my favor. Although at the time, 1941, bad cuts were rarely enough to stop a fight. I waited till the ref was on the opposite side of the ring and couldn't see me, and I landed a powerful blow, which landed solidly below Harrison's belt. It seemed logical to me that this would slow him down, and give me more time to recover and get to my corner where Paulie would try to stop the bleeding, which was hampering my vision and burning my eyes.

Although Harrison and his corner (and many fans) complained loudly, the referee didn't see the punch so he didn't warn me or try to stop the fight, or even caution me. My strategy although illegal, worked, and I was able to finish out the round and I had the feeling that I had now evened up the score from our first fight. Although I now had one heck of a pounding in my brain, I was going to be able to continue. But Bob Harrison had succeeded in giving me two headaches in two fights.

Between rounds Paulie worked feverishly trying to close the cut, but it didn't seem to help very much. "It isn't that bad", he lied, "but because it's over your eye, you won't be able to see very clearly for long, you're going to have to end the fight in this round. Do whatever it takes, Tony, or you're going to have a lot of problems in the later rounds." He didn't seem to realize that I wasn't seeing clearly even then, or didn't care, and I didn't want to tell him that for fear he'd try to throw in the towel to stop the fight.

Since I figured that Bob Harrison started the illegal stuff, I made up my mind to continue to fight dirty also. It was one bit of advice from Paulie that I really didn't need now.

The bell rang to start round eight rang. We met at center ring. Harrison decided that since I was unable to see much out of my right eye, he was going to go after the cut and end the fight quickly. Instead of the crouch he now fought straight up again, constantly working his glove into the cut and badly compounding my headache as well as my vision problems.

As soon as I could see that the referee was way out of position, I landed a solid uppercut to Harrison's groin. He doubled over in pain giving me the only chance I felt that I was going to have left. When Harrison was bending forward in pain, I landed a powerful right uppercut on his chin, and Harrison was finished. The ref obviously knew he that wasn't going to make the count, and waved it off and lifted my hand in victory to a very loud and unhappy pro Harrison crowd. Whatever the fans had on hand they threw into the ring. It was similar to my last fight, except this time they weren't trying to hurt each other; they were only going after my team of Paulie, Billy and me.

Fortunately there was a large contingent of the men in blue on hand, so it was quickly brought under control and no full-fledged riot erupted.

It was a rough trip, with a large police escort, to our dressing room. While we were there we asked for the police to remain and guard the door, and take us out to Paulies' old beat up black Ford that was awaiting us in the parking lot. They agreed and after my shower, we escaped quickly, ducking most of the large variety of items that the unhappy crowd was raining down upon us. Paulie drove us to the hospital where I received 17 stitches to close the cut.

Mom was told to stay at home for this fight, because of her health, and that was a good thing as we knew she would be completely safe. Uncle Johnny finally made it out of the arena when the angry crowd departed, not knowing he was with us.

The crowd, many of whom saw the low blow, started screaming for my head, as the three of us reached the safety of the car. Some even tried to break the windows and kick in the sides of Paulie's car, but the police were able to hold them at bay, at least until we took off. Paulie almost ran over one of them who stupidly jumped in front of the car, but Paulie swerved in the nick of time.

Driving home from the hospital, Paulie told Billy and me. "Great work, Tony! While I don't approve of dirty fighting, he started it with the head butt, and if you didn't do exactly what you did. You would have been hurt a lot worse and you would have also lost the fight."

But I had won the most important fight of my life, and that should have been all that really mattered. It was to Billy, Paulie and Uncle Johnny, but I just wasn't satisfied. I wanted to prove I could win on my natural ability, not on a foul. I was actually feeling guilty. I still wanted to win legitimately.

"Forget it, Tony", Paulie said. "Figure it this way, your next opponent isn't going to try to win on a foul. You showed them it wasn't worth the price that they would have to pay for the effort."

Paulie had a good point. But I still felt pangs of guilt.

A third match was then scheduled between Bob Harrison and myself. The rules were fairly simple, there were no rules. It was to be a grudge match between the two of us, and there was plenty of money to be made. The offer that was made to me by the promoter was very tempting. It was winner take all. But I turned it down. All I wanted was a fair fight, not a fight to the finish. The Harrison camp called me a 'fucking coward,' but I wasn't at all interested in their opinion of me. If he was going to fight me again, it would be no fouls, even if it took more than one referee.

So instead we proposed a third fight, with two referees to prevent fouls, and a winner take all purse. But an intentional foul call would result in an immediate disqualification. After a few weeks I learned that this was acceptable to the Harrison camp. But with just one referee that would be agreed upon by all of us, and in a neutral arena.

Paulie didn't like the idea. He simply didn't trust Harrison, but knowing there would a neutral referee officiating, he gave in. Mom liked the idea, because she felt that I would be relatively safe, and Billy, well all he seemed to care about was that he wanted to fight again on the undercard. It was a request that would never again be a problem for us to honor.

Uncle Johnny didn't like the idea of a fair fight. He, as well as most of the crowd in attendance, loved all those roughhouse tactics. "It's what brings out the crowd", he would say. "They want to see as much blood as possible. Ya give em a boring fight, they won't pay to see ya fight again."

Funny, I thought the name of the game was hit and not be hit. Wasn't that how Willie Pep fought? Wasn't that why the sport of boxing was termed the "sweet science?"

The final match between Harrison and myself happened eight weeks after our previous encounter. My cut had not quite healed as much as I would have liked, but I didn't let on, and besides, I had to honor the contract. And I wanted this to be my chance to win the third match fair and square.

Right before the fight, Bob Harrison came into my dressing room and held out his hand in a gesture of friendship. He said he was going to show everyone that he could whup my white ass without resorting to fouls, and that the only way I was going to beat him was by fighting dirty, and if I did, he'd get the decision and the purse. I knew this was part of the head game he was playing, and yet he seemed to be a really a nice guy outside the ring, but could I trust him when the bell sounded?

I shook his hand, but told him that if he kept it clean, so would I, and may the best man win.

"That, of course, no doubt will be me!" Harrison said, smiling confidently as he turned and went back to his dressing room.

It was strange, I knew that Bob Harrison was a dirty fighter, yet, I genuinely liked the guy and for some reason, I had the utmost respect for him. I honestly felt that we could easily become friends, if we knew each other outside the ring.

As before, Billy was to be on the undercard, only this time he was in the semi-main. He didn't really want that because he wanted to be in my corner in case any trouble were to arise. We worked it out so there would be an intermission between his bout and mine, and that Billy would still be able to have time to work my corner after his fight.

He fought in a six round bout against a far more experienced club fighter. But the time had long past when Billy ever feared anyone and it took him two and a half rounds to knockout his opponent, which was longer than he generally took with most fighters. With his boyish good looks and tremendous power punching, he had become a real fan favorite as well.

He came back to the dressing room, took a quick shower, and after a few minutes walked with me and Paulie down the dark aisle to the ring, carrying the spit bucket as well as my mouthpiece.

Harrison and I didn't touch gloves after the introduction, it wasn't required by the rules, and neither of us were really completely sure that we could trust the other.

Strangely enough, this truly was a boxing match, the way the sport was meant to be. There were no intentional fouls and no disqualification, just pure give and take boxing. It was a war and Harrison and I gave it our all. We both were staggered a few times, but neither of us went down.

The bout went the full ten round distance, with the referee raising both our hands at the end of the contest to signify a draw. The ref would also have to score the fights in Philadelphia and other cities in those days. The crowd roared loudly in approval of the decision and again the call went out for a rematch. We split the entire purse 50-50, which certainly seemed fair enough to both of us.

Midway through the bout, I threw an uppercut that landed slightly south of the border, as Harrison was wearing his trunks pretty high. It was obviously unintentional, and although the ref did warn me, he knew it wasn't done with bad intentions. I actually felt bad about it and put out my glove and said "Sorry" and Harrison touched gloves, also realizing that it was not intentional and did not respond with a low blow in return.

After the fight we hugged each other as a form of congratulations and although the crowd and promoters wanted it, we never fought each other again. We respected each other and would become fast friends in the years that would follow.

Chapter IV

It was the summer of 1943, and the tide of WWII had shifted at the battle of Midway, in the Pacific, when the American Navy routed the Imperial Japanese fleet. The Germans were in full retreat from Russia, having failed to handle the cold Russian winter. They were killing at will as they went, and burning as much of the land and buildings as they could in their rapid retreat back to safer ground. From this came the term "scorched earth policy". They had suffered enormous losses in their unsuccessful attempt to conquer Russia with a surprise attack, early the previous winter.

After a number of bloody battles, Italy would surrender a year later, and Mussolini would be given his just reward, captured and killed in Milan, and strung up by his heels, by the Partisans. The Fascist Party was out of power.

There were many race riots going on in major American cities, and President Roosevelt had frozen wages, salaries and prices in an effort to keep control of our still very soft economy.

I was now 20, and had temporarily dropped out of college. I had come to learn that I had to attend college full time to be allowed to box in school, and instead I chose to pursue a full time boxing career. Mom had taken seriously ill, and both of the Petrovic boys had no choice but to bring home the bacon.

I was very tempted to join the military. But while Uncle Johnny thought it would do me a world of good, and that "everyone should be proud to do their duty and to serve their country, better men than you and I have died for it." He also felt that it was more important now for me to earn a living, as mom, who was growing ever more frail, needed me around to take care of her. So I decided to try to earn a living through boxing. Mom would never find out that I had dropped out of Penn State. I made sure of that, but I also promised myself that I was going to continue my college education after I quit boxing. Looking back, a lot of guys felt that way, but never continued their education. I was the exception to that rule, I'm proud to say.

Billy also had made up his mind to quit school, and despite mom's loud protest at first, he, in fact, did, while telling her that he had decided to remain in school. It was a lie, but one both Billy and I felt comfortable with. Why not let mom die happy? The truth could only hurt her.

Billy continued to fight on a regular basis, and remained undefeated with a knockout streak of 11 KO's in 11 fights. And he also kept pushing Paulie to try to get him a title shot. Paulie kept refusing, saying Billy just 'didn't have enough experience, yet'.

Without the title shot, Billy became more and more withdrawn. He tried to enlist in the Army, but he was turned down because of his 'attitude'. I wasn't sure exactly what that meant. It was probably the right decision on their part, as Billy still carried this very large and growing chip on his shoulder. And if Uncle Sam turned him down when volunteers were badly needed, I figured that my little brother must have had a far worse emotional problem than anyone of us had ever thought.

Billy really enjoyed fighting. It was a good outlet for his frustrations, but it seemed that his matches just didn't happen often enough to ease that cold-blooded streak he had garnered. So he continued going to the gym and at times even sold newspapers or pencils and sometimes fruit on the street corner to earn a few extra dollars. He never was a guy who liked to stay home. He had also become very superstitious about a number of things. He would never walk under a ladder. I never figured out where that came from though. No one in the Petrovic family was superstitious as far as I knew.

Billy really loved boxing and told me that he hated doing the other menial work, which he found very boring, but he was all too aware that the family now needed money very badly to help pay mom's ever increasing medical bills. She had lost a lot of weight and we were grateful to be able to get some used clothes from some of our friends from the Church, who gladly pitched it. They would even come over a couple of times a week with full cardboard cartons to make sure we had plenty of food. Billy resented this because he felt that we didn't need charity, but never pushed the issue because he didn't want to upset mom, He was very pleasant to all the donors, outwardly.

I suppose that I could have done the same work as Billy. Unlike my younger brother, I wasn't too proud to stand on the corner and peddle whatever I could. But everyone kept telling me that I could earn far more money in boxing as a top contender or a world champion, which I was sure to become. They told me to dedicate all of my spare time and energy to training and fighting. I listened, and did what was asked of me, but I somehow felt like I was letting the family down.

Uncle Johnny also was in and out of the hospital, and now had tubes running into his nose from a large oxygen tank on a metal roller, placed near his favorite seat in the house, facing the TV and alongside that old Philco radio he loved so much. Aunt Jen, as always, was by his side, ever loyal and anxious to meet his every need.

I had moved steadily up the ladder in the ratings. I was now ranked among the top 10 middleweights in the world, (I think is was 7th) with a record of 16-1, with 1 draw, but only nine knockouts. These were really TKO's, that I usually got by wearing down my opponents. Unlike Billy, I was never a one-punch knockout artist. Although there were many times I wish that I were. I had to train harder because in the ring, I always had to work harder.

One afternoon Paulie called Billy and I into his office in the gym. He told us in no uncertain terms that he had sold our contracts (standard ones with 15% going to Paulie) to a Mr. Grabowski, and that Grabowski would be handling our careers from that moment on. Paulie said, "I'm sorry boys, he just made me an offer that I couldn't refuse." At that point, we didn't ask Paulie what he meant by that, and, looking back, I know now that we should have.

At first we balked at the managerial change. We did owe Paulie a lot and we trusted him completely. We wanted to remain loyal to him. But, when Mr. G, as he had come to be known to us as, showed us the potential we had to make lots more money in the ring. We were pair of brothers boxing and winning which was somewhat rare in those days. The problem that Billy and I had was that he wanted 40% and with the percentage we would give Paulie, we'd be making less than Mr. G. did.

In truth a world champion brother team is just about as rare in today's sport, with even more competition. Yeah the Spinks brothers pulled it off, but Leon's win proved to be little more than a flash in the pan, and he didn't stay at or near the top very long.

So we had a tough decision to make. What we didn't know at the time was that Mr. G. was going to try to run our careers completely, tell us not only who to fight, but when to win or lose. And take the money we needed to take care of mom. Fortunately it never came down to that.

With mom being very ill, the family needed the money badly, so we decided that maybe Paulie could be right, or at least I did. Billy really didn't seem to care either way; all he ever wanted to do was fight and hurt his opponent, that was his life. So the money didn't really seem to matter to him as long as he kept fighting regularly and winning. In truth, we both felt like we were being treated like a piece of old, raw meat, something to be chewed up and discarded, We felt that we had now had no choice, so we went along with it. Whatever happened to the word loyalty, I wondered?

At our first and only meeting with Mr. G., at Paulie's Gym (Paulie was elsewhere). We saw that Mr. G. was a very heavyset guy with a lot of gold teeth; and wavy grey hair and mustache. He was wearing a dark double-breasted suit, which had a noticeable bulge underneath the suit's right breast. He wore a dark fedora hat, and a red tie with a gold tie pin in the shape of a boxing glove, and hard brown, horn-rimmed sunglasses. He spoke with a distinct Boston accent. Mr. G was not a very pleasant guy to talk to, as he had pointed brown teeth and bad breath. He swore an awful lot. Billy and I took an instant dislike to him, although Billy didn't really pay that much intention. His mind always seemed to wander.

Mr. G. insisted, in no uncertain terms, that we would continue to do all our training at Paulie's Gym, but also made it very clear that our management was no longer going to be in Paulie's hands. He pointed out to us, by loosening the button on his suit and revealing the stock of a pistol, that he was now going to be totally in charge. He had purchased our contracts, and he 'now owned us lock, stock and barrel, and 'we had to fight for him and follow his instructions to the letter, or he would make sure that we would never fight again at all', as he put it.

After we left, Billy told me that "That guy is full of it! Who the hell does he think he is? It sounded like a threat 'and he isn't about to get away with threatening us.' To be sure, Billy was not the type of a person you'd ever want to threaten or even imply a threat. But after a long conversation, while walking home, I made clear to Billy that although it was indeed a threat, that with mom being very ill, our choices seemed to be pretty limited to slim and none, and slim and had left town. It was either work for Mr. G, or resort to selling apples, pencils or newspapers on the street corner for just pennies a day. Boxing was the obvious choice. Billie wanted to go back to tell Grabowski to shove it up his ass and rip up the contract, but I was able to cool him down.

"George Grabowski?" Uncle Johnny jumped out of his chair, coughing, banging into and almost knocking over his oxygen tank, yelled, when we told him the news. "You can't fight for him. He's tied in with the underworld big time. He's the type of scum that would probably kill his own mother just for a laugh. He's a fucking scumbag. (I don't think we had ever heard Johnny curse before). He's a damn no-good mobster! You can't have this smear on our family name. Petrovic is a name to be proud of. What would your father think? Besides, the Feds are investigating Grabowski now. They think that he fixes some of the fights. Think? I wouldn't be at all surprised if he fixed all of them! I've heard a lot of bad things about him, including that he's had people who cross him killed. You certainly don't want to be mixed up with this guy kids, believe me".

"Wait a second. What in God's name does that have to do with us, Uncle Johnny?" I inquired. "We're certainly not going to become gangsters. Hell we've never even stolen a piece of candy, (I knew that I didn't but I wasn't that sure about Billy) and we have never been in on any fixes and never would be. Uncle Johnny, you know us way better than that. The family name will always be safe in our hands."

Uncle Johnny sat down slowly and coughed loudly a few more times, and spit some brown fluid into a gold metal container on the floor next to him. It was obvious that all this excitement was not very good for him "You just don't understand! That's not the issue here, boys. Dollars to doughnuts that sleezeball is going to tell you how and when to win and how and when you're supposed to lose. You will not have any say in it. These mobsters bet heavily on the fight and they don't like to lose. If you fight for him, sooner or later, you're going to have to take a dive. Probably sooner. The feds are looking into the stories of fixed matches now! Don't do it! Keep your pride. It's all dirty money and it's just not worth it! You have the Petrovic name to think about, and that's the most important thing to any of us."

"No way that's ever going to happen, Uncle Johnny," Billy laughed. All I'm going to do is to fight and win like I always do, by knockout. Nothing can or will ever change that! There's just no way this Grabowski asshole, or anyone else in the entire world, is going to make me or Tony lose a fight. You can rest easy. The Petrovic name is safe with us. We'd rather die than dishonor the family."

Billy looked at me for approval, but I wasn't quite as sure as he was about being willing to lay down my life to protect the family name. In war yes, but not in boxing. I just quietly nodded.

"Billy, listen to me damn it. Between the both of you, you haven't been around as long as I have. You haven't seen what really goes on in this world!" Uncle Johnny said slowly. "Guys like George Grabowski, they play for keeps. Even though they've never been nailed, at least not yet, everyone knows that they're cold-blooded killers and you can't cross them. They could and will kill you without thinking twice about it if you cross them. I've heard plenty of stories about this Grabowski guy. I hear he always carries a gun and is not afraid to use it. He's a real scumbag."

Billy and I stood back and looked at each other. We had seen the gun.

I stood back quietly and listened very intently to the loud conversation between Billy and Uncle Johnny, growing more and more confused, I was now wondering what we should do next. I made up my mind that the only person who could give us good advice and tell us what to really expect, at this point, was Paulie. After all he was the guy who was responsible for doing this to us in the first place, and who, fortunately I thought, was still going to be training us in his gym. "I think it's time we sat down with Paulie and find out what the hell is really going on," I said, looking at Billy. "Good idea boys, but tell him you want the straight scoop on MR. G. We both put on our hats and coats and headed straight to the gym.

"I'm sorry kids, I hate to tell ya this, but Your Uncle Johnny is absolutely correct," Paulie, shook his head and looked down at the wooden floor, said to us after we explained what Johnny had just told us. Paulie simply shook his head. "You don't want to cross this guy or your boxing careers could be over, or even worse, your lives. He's not a very nice man, and he has ties to the mob. Hell, some people even think he's one of the head honchos. Do you really think he gave me a choice when he offered to buy out your contracts"

Billy and I sat quietly for awhile, wondering what the hell we had gotten ourselves into, or more to the point, what Paulie had gotten us into, and why. What had we done to him, except follow his instructions, win and allow him to make 1/3 of our purse as well? But like Paulie said, he probably didn't have much choice. Maybe none.

"Why the hell would you want to sell us out? You were supposed to be our friend. We trusted you. You brought us along this far just to sell us out?" I inquired.

"I am your friend, you must know that or you certainly wouldn't have come here now, and I'm truly sorry, but it's not like I had a whole lot of choice, boys. He made me an offer, and not a very good one, but you just don't say 'no' to Mr. G. and live to tell about it." Paulie hesitated, "But I'll tell you what I will do. Let me speak to him again, and tell him that you told me that you won't fight at all, unless you fight to win. You may not have to take a dive, although it might very well mean that a couple of your opponents will be going into the tank instead, but it's better than losing. And when you have earned enough money maybe you can buy out your contracts and be free and independent. I don't know if talking to Grabowski will help the situation, in truth, it probably won't, but it certainly can't hurt".

A few days later, when we showed up at the gym for our workout, Paulie called us over to his desk and whispered "You kids are really very lucky. The Feds, who are investigating Mr. G. from top to bottom, are causing him to lay low now. And he told me that at least for the time being, I'm back to managing you. He even put your contracts back in my name, so nothing could ever be traced back to either of us. I think that maybe it's going to work out for the best."

"Now just keep in mind that can all change again, and quickly, if he doesn't go to the pen, or if he changes his mind, which he's been known to do quite often. Hell, you kids may have just gotten real lucky. He could have even easily have sold your contracts to another mobster who the feds weren't looking at yet and he didn't. Maybe he likes you or maybe he didn't get the right offer for ya. But right now Mr. G. HAS TO keep his nose clean. He has no other choice. In short, for the time being, the contract you had with him is broken and no one is ever supposed to know anything about it. Make sure your entire family knows that. We don't want to create any extra problems for this guy! This whole incident, it never happened! Got it?

Of course Paulie then told us that it was only a verbal contract, anyway, and as I learned later, a written contract was exactly what the Feds were looking for, and Paulie had destroyed that, or said he did, as he obviously had good cause to fear Grabowski and his cronies. We never signed the old or any new contract, and I can only assume that Paulie never did either, because when Mr. G went to trial and eventually to jail, where he was eventually murdered, we were hardly mentioned by the Feds, although we were called upon to testify to the 'nothing' that we knew. Our memory of this entire incident was intentionally gone.

Billy and I breathed a loud sigh of relief. What could have easily been the end of our budding ring careers or even our young lives. We had been taken care of, at least for the time being. We needed those careers desperately to take care of mom, who had now been diagnosed, correctly this time, with terminal breast cancer and we were told she would have no more than three more months to live. Still, the medical bills were continuing to pile up.

The doctor, who was a family friend, asked us on the qt if we wanted mom to be revived if she went into a coma and if we wanted her to spend her final days at home. There was no such thing as a living will at that time, but the doctor had always taken care of the Petrovic family and didn't want to see mom suffer more than she had to. We spoke to mom about it, and she didn't want to be kept on life support, nor did she want to be a burden to the family if she were to return home, although it would keep down the medical bill from the hospital. We told the doctor this and then returned home to give the grim news to the rest of the family.

We went home and also told Uncle Johnny the news about Grabowski, and to say that he was relieved would be a gross understatement. "Great news, boys, thank the Good Lord for his never-ending kindness" was all he would say. He didn't say anything about mom's decision, as it was obviously too stressful for him to deal with. Johnny was all for family.

Paulie began to take extra good care of us now, because he felt that we were going to be his main meal ticket, and probably wanted to make as much as he could in case Mr. G. or one of his cohorts returned. He willingly honored our request that we only fight on the same cards, because of our ever-growing popularity, we would always be a big plus for at the gate for everyone involved. However, he often mentioned that we could draw twice as many fans if we fought separately. We'll never know if he was right or wrong about that.

In May 1943, Billy and I had our first fights of the year at an arena in Buffalo, New York. We were matched against a couple of local Hispanic kids, who, judging by their strong ring records were on the way up the boxing ladder.

Paulie told Billy and I his standard advice, to look for the quick knockout because we might not be able to win a decision in our opponent's hometown.

It was our biggest payday to date, and I was promised a shot at the middleweight title down the road, if I won my fight.

I asked about Billy, but Paulie said because of all his early knockouts, he really doesn't have the ring experience, round wise, to fight for the bauble yet. "How can he fight a 15 round fight, if he's hardly fought much more than 15 rounds in his whole career yet?" It was a logical question. It seemed that Billy's power may well have proved to be his undoing. But we were told that if I got the title shot, he still would be fighting on the undercard. And that if he had enough rounds under his belt, by the time I got my shot at the crown, Billy probably would also get a chance to fight for a title shortly thereafter.

I didn't like the idea; although I also felt that he was too raw, Billy was just couldn't find anyone to fight who had a solid chin, and who could give him enough rounds to enable him to fight for the title. But I went along with it because at the least we would be fighting on the same card, and we always split our purses, so Billy would never be shortchanged.

This was to be one of the toughest fights of my career. The guy I was in with was a tall, rangy, experienced fighter who had won all his 16 fights by knockout. On the opposite side of the coin, he also had been knocked out in every one of his four losses. This guy was one of those guys who either knocks you out, or you knock him out. There seemed to be no way that his fights could ever end in a decision.

Billy drew a kid who had 11 wins in 12 fights, and was viewed as a defensive fighter who was also an excellent counter puncher, He did his best work fighting off the ropes. 'Defensive' and 'off the ropes' are two terms that are rarely used today, since few trainers teach defense or counter punching. This is probably because the vast majority of today's fans want the fast action and the knockout, rarely provided by counter-punchers. It would be a good match for Billy because this guy was supposed to have a solid chin, and Billy needed the extra rounds.

It was to be an outdoor fight, in an old baseball stadium, held during the day, and Paulie said the place was sold out, in anticipation of seeing Billy and I. We both seemed to be sure-fire future world champions. But, he cautioned, don't let that go to your head and get careless. Billy didn't have to worry about his opponent's power, he didn't have much, but I knew that I certainly was going to have my hands full.

Both Uncle Johnny and mom couldn't attend these fights. It was just too far for them to travel, and neither was in very good health. It was the first but not the last of our fights that they missed. In fact, mom only saw us once, in the ring again, when we fought for the title, and that was only because it was on TV. Uncle Johnny was able to make most of the fights we fought in Philly, which now, because of our records, had become more and more infrequent. And Johnny always had to be within reach of his oxygen tank.

We were very grateful however, that a lot of our hometown fans had traveled to upstate New York to root us on. At least we knew it wasn't entirely enemy territory, but we also knew not to expect to win a decision.

"Stick and move. Keep him off balance with your jab," that was Paulie's instructions that he gave to me as he wrapped my hands in the dressing room. "Don't be a stationary target, you have to keep that head moving. This Rodriguez kid you're fighting, throws a powerful overhand right, and if it lands solid the fight could be over very quickly. This maybe your chance at a title shot as well. So keep that left hand high at all times, protect your chin and look for the opening that he'll give you sooner or later, if you work the body right."

It was a very hot and humid day by Buffalo standards, with no breeze blowing, and we didn't have to work up a sweat to get loose, we sweated a lot just walking to the ring. But of course, we had already loosened up in the dressing room.

Billy's opponent was a Cuban guy named Dino Mercado, and he was very fast, the type of fighter you had to catch to hit. It took Billy eight rounds of the scheduled ten rounder to finally catch up to him in his corner and unleash a fusillade of heavy punches. The kid slipped a lot of them, but it only took a short combination from Billy to cause Mercado's legs to sag. His corner quickly tossed in the towel in defeat, although he never actually hit the canvas. And he didn't protest to his corner at all. He knew they had probably saved his ring career.

It was a very good fight for Billy because he got in some of the extra rounds and experience that Paulie had said he needed. He kept his undefeated and knockout streak intact as well.

I'm not sure how the referee had scored the fight up till then. I thought Billy was winning, but I also knew that many of the rounds were very close, as Billy was never that good a boxer, and a hometown decision was not out of the question, in fact, it was probably very likely.

Billy was awarded a TKO, a technical knockout, and the first non one-punch knockout of his young career, although if the fight went any longer, there's little doubt that he would have kept his KO streak intact. But going the eight rounds had given him that extra experience he needed that would help to garner him a future title fight.

Now it was my turn, and I really didn't feel that strong, as the heat and humidity, rare for that time of year in New York State, had taken somewhat of a toll on me. These were the worst conditions to date that I had ever fought in. I felt wilted and my energy was almost drained by the time the first bell sounded.

My opponent, Jorge Rivera, was a bit taller than me, and by his muscle tone, looked more like a bodybuilder instead of a boxer. These were the kind of guys, Paulie had said were 'very slow because they were all muscle bound.' The way I was wilting, and seeing those bulging biceps, I hoped that Paulie was right.

We touched gloves after the introduction, and met in center-ring. The first round was just feeling each other out, seeking the strengths and weaknesses of the other and looking for openings. I was glad Paulie was in my corner, because I sure couldn't see any openings to take advantage of.

In round two, Rivera hit me with an overhand right, which I still remember till this day. I hit the canvas, and don't remember making it up by the time the ref counted to ten. Fortunately it was at the end of the round, and I was saved by the bell, and I got a much-needed breather while sitting on the stool in my corner. I was so out of it I began walking to the wrong corner. This Rivera guy wasn't slow, even with all his muscles.

Paulie poured ice water over my pounding head and then poured ice down the front of my trunks. It revived me enough to barely be able to pay attention to his instructions and held on for most of round three, till I was able to get my legs, which felt like spaghetti for a short time, back under me. I was lucky because my opponent was over-confident and had no intention of trying to end the fight that early. He probably either didn't realize that I wasn't one hundred percent, or he just didn't care and wanted the work. Or, maybe he was over confidant. His reasons didn't matter. It was a mistake. He allowed me to remain in the fight and that was going to cost him dearly.

I was back to normal, so to speak, and the legs got stronger in round four, and the following five rounds were pretty even. He was now looking for the one big shot, and I was banging away at his body as Paulie instructed, trying to slow him down and bring down his guard. I was landing more punches, but he had definitely been landing the harder ones. I knew that I'd be pissing blood for awhile after the fight.

Paulie told me that he thought the fight was just about even when I sat down to await the final round. "But", he said, "he knocked you down and this is Rivera's home town, and I doubt you'll get any decision here. You probably need a knockout. He's tired and he's dropping his left hand a bit. Find an opening and go for the one big punch. Set up your right hand and turn it

119

over. You've worked his body plenty and he's starting to drop his guard. This may be your last chance to avoid the loss."

Sounded like great advice, but it was much easier said than done. It wasn't Paulie in the ring, it was me, and the heat and humidity had taken a toll and I didn't think I had enough strength left in the tank to even last half a round. And since Rivera was from the area, I assumed he was used to the conditions and was sure to get the decision.

Fortunately for me, Rivera, who was missing a lot of his big punches, didn't have much left in his tank either. He came out for round ten and we touched gloves in a show of mutual respect. I circled him, looking for the one opening that would give me the KO I was sure that I needed. Rivera's hands were low and his chin looked to be an easy target, but I needed the chance and enough energy to reach that inviting mark.

That chance I was looking for came midway through the round, when Rivera, going for the knockout, threw a wild right hand, that sailed over my left ear. When he threw the punch, he dropped his left hand guard just enough to provide me the small opening that I needed. It was like manna from Heaven. I knew it could be my only chance. I threw a quick left to his stomach which made him wince, and followed it up with an overhand right to his jaw, and I watched in amazement as his knees crumbled. He landed flat, face down on the canvas. I was standing over him, when the ref stepped in and told me to go to a neutral corner. I was a bit confused and went to my own, where Paulie was yelling and motioning to me, but it was the ref, who had not started to count yet, who motioned me to go to a different ring post. Which I finally understood. I wasn't used to knocking down my opponents, so this instinct which was natural to most fighters, was not to me.

By some great stroke of luck, even with the extra time given to him before the count started, Rivera could only make it to his knees, with his eyes still rolled back in this head, when the ref tolled ten and waved the fight over. The heat and humidity may have also added to his weakened condition. I sure didn't think it was my power. But I didn't know and really didn't care. Billy and Paulie quickly jumped into the ring to hug me, but I was just too exhausted to do much in return. Just having the ref raise my hand in victory was a chore, and I couldn't wait to get back to the shade of the dressing room and out of the blazing hot sun. The thought of a cold shower motivated me more now, than the knockout did.

After having my hand raised and congratulating Jorge Rivera, who looked fine, except for a large mouse under his left eye, on the fine fight he put up, we picked up our gear and headed to the dressing room.

I don't even know how I made it back. I was pretty well banged up and totally exhausted and Paulie kept giving me a lot of liquids to drink in order to recover. Paulie even talked about getting me to a hospital for a transfusion. Believe me, it took a good couple of hours before I felt strong enough to get dressed, let alone leave the stadium. In all my ring years, I don't ever remember being that bruised and tired. I felt entirely limp and listless.

I vaguely remember begging Paulie to never allow me to fight outside in the heat again. Paulie, as always would just grunt and smile. I never knew if he was really paying attention to me or not. I knew that it didn't matter, because if the money were there, he'd have me in the ring, even if the fight was going to be held outdoors, in the middle of a desert.

But right then, it seemed like the Petrovic brothers would soon be fighting in the same ring on the same night for both the welterweight and middleweight world titles.

But the legal problems with Mr. G. and the Feds, wasn't quite over just yet.

Paulie had been called to testify before the Federal Sub Commission in Washington DC that was investigating organized crime in professional sports, and while he was only there to answer some questions, Billy's and my name somehow came up during that hearing. And although there were no charges going to be filed against Paulie, or us, we had gone to DC with him, and were to testify separately, and weren't quite sure what to expect when he finally arrived back to our hotel.

Speaking of heat and humidity, our nation's capitol, in the summertime, was far from the best place to feel comfortable. You could work up a sweat just by opening a hotel window.

But at least we didn't have to fight there.

And, since our names did come up when the Feds were questioning Paulie, Billy and I were called to testify and we all told the truth, except for the contract with Mr. G. that no one was ever supposed to know about, which we omitted. Paulie was excused early from testifying, so he left us with instructions to tell the Feds that we never had one fight for Mr. G. and never signed a contract, which was true. Paulie packed his bags and drove back home to Philadelphia.

We had to put on our Sunday best, and go to the Senate Office Building on Capitol Hill to testify. It was fairly easy, all we did was tell the truth, as we knew it. It only took a few hours and Billy and I soon were on a Greyhound bus and on our way back to Philly, and the gym, where we knew Paulie was going to be waiting, anxious to hear if we gave away any extra information. We didn't'. We really didn't have much to give, anyhow.

"Sorry, I really had to mention your names, guys", Paulie began. "But all I did was tell the truth. That at no time was a contract signed between me, or you two, with Mr. G. It's all over now and he'll probably be going to stand trial. I bet he's probably going to be spending a lot of time in the big house."

Although we were very naïve and didn't really know what the 'big house' was at that time, we assumed it wasn't a good place to be.

We hadn't changed our clothes yet, although they had become very sticky from our trip. So we went home, showered, changed, and went to visit mom in the hospital. She was looking even thinner than before we had left, and her cough had gotten worse and had become more like a wheeze. No matter how much money we had made and spent for her treatment, there was still no cure, and all the doctors and nurses could do was make her comfortable. Nothing had to be said. We all knew that it was just a matter of time, and there wasn't much time left.

But we never could understand (and still can't) that with all the advancement in medicine, why no one had ever found a cure for cancer, even till this day. Billy thought they had one, but kept it secret because there was just too much money for the doctors and charities out there, to make that knowledge public. Besides a lot of folks felt that we didn't need over-population and that this was a way to keep the numbers down. I didn't feel that way at all, but really had no good argument against the way that Billy felt. If he was right, mom might have been saved or at least prolonged. I guess it was just a matter of prospective, and cynicism.

We kissed mom on the cheek, and headed to Uncle Johnny, who had already heard the big news. And it was all over the sports page of the local and probably national newspapers, Billy and I were indeed going to get a title shot if we kept on winning. Uncle Johnny was also very pleased. Seems that the media had found out before Paulie or we did.

And although we met the conditions and continued to win, those promised title shots, however, wouldn't come until November, 1945, and we had a long wait, and a lot more training to do before that.

But for the next few months, Billy and I would pretty much take it easy, and just run a few miles a day and do some sit-ups and push-ups. No sparring was required of us. It was like a vacation, which Billy said he didn't want or need, but that was Billy. With the money we made in our Buffalo fights, it was easy for me to enjoy a much more comfortable lifestyle.

During that period, when we weren't together, which wasn't very often, Billy had found a girlfriend. I'm not sure where he had met her, although he probably had told me and I've long since forgotten. She was a cute little long haired, redheaded gal with brown eyes, freckles and a turned up nose, named Mary Sue Johnson. And to me she seemed to be every bit as sweet as she looked.

Paulie thought she was just a hanger-on, and that all Mary Sue wanted was Billy's money, that he was sure to make, and to be around a great up and coming fighter and a future world champion. Paulie had been around the fight game a long time, and had married and divorced three times, so he was always very cynical about things like this. He was the same way about fighters and their lack of loyalty to those who brought them to the top.

And Paulie was adamant that there would if there was sex between Billy and his new girl friend, it would be up till six weeks before fight time, and after that, all work and no play for my younger brother.

Billy however did not feel the same way that Paulie did. He had fallen in love with Mary Sue. In fact Paulie once told me that 'Billy was too damn innocent and was going to be taken to the cleaners". But despite Paulie's skepticism, Billy soon began to talk to me about giving Mary Sue an engagement ring.

"How long have you known Mary?" I inquired.

"About three years now," Billy responded, "But we've only been going out together seriously for a couple of months now. You're not going to give me a hard time also, are you, Tony?"

"Well, I do think that you're a little too young right now. Have you set a date? Who's going to marry you two?" I asked. "And where? You can't get married in Philly. You have to be twenty one".

"We're going to elope, I think and then have a regular church wedding later on. I was thinking about taking her to Tijuana, or Nevada, but Mary didn't like the idea. We're both sixteen and I think that there are some places in the South like Arkansas, where we can go and legally get married now. Mary's only three months younger than me. Besides, I'm just talking engagement now, not marriage. Not yet, anyway. And Mary Sue's the real McCoy, Tony. I'm not waiting till I'm twenty one to get her in the sack, and she intends to remain a virgin till we get married. Her upbringing is not much different from ours. But that's the problem with being into religion like she is. It's great for some, but for me at least, I think it's a serious drawback."

I had only spoken to Mary a few times before, but never thought about her as being my future sister in law. There could be no doubt, however, that Billy was deeply in love with her, because his behavior had changed again, and he now always seemed to be happy, that is until he set foot into the boxing ring. And then, the only thing that would make him really happy was a pier six brawl ending in a knockout, by him of course.

Paulie had warned both of us on many occasions, about not having sex at least six weeks before a fight, and certainly not the two weeks before. "It will definitely weaken you", he cautioned.

It really wasn't an issue for me, since I was not seeing anyone at the time. And the only fire in my belly was to keep on training hard and winning fights. I had to make enough money to take care of mom's ever mounting medical bills and to continue to donate money to try to help the scientists find a cure for cancer. Of course they still haven't found one to this day. Sometimes I wonder if Billy was right. Is this is really progress? I know that they've found a few things to help the suffering, but no cures.

At the time, seeing how happy Billy had now become, I began to give some thought about finding a girlfriend also. But, unlike Billy, I never socialized very much, and even though I wanted to find that special someone, I wasn't ready to go looking for her just yet. If it happened, it happened. Sure I had a normal interest in sex, but I guess my religious beliefs prevented me from acting on it.

Paulie was always asking Billy if he was having sex with Mary, and he simply shook his head and said, "not that it's any of your damn business, Paulie, but she wants to remain a virgin until she gets married."

"Do you?" Paulie inquired of him. Billy turned away, never answering him.

So, I don't know if Paulie believed that or not (Billy said he had told me it was the truth), because Paulie continue to warn us about it.

In any event, we were scheduled for a November fight at Forbes Field in Pittsburgh, a major league baseball stadium where the Pirates played. The stadium had lights, so we could fight in the evening. However that fight date had to be postponed, because mom had passed away a few days earlier and we obviously insisted on attending the funeral and being allowed to grieve. There were no repercussions, but even if they were, it wouldn't have changed our decision.

The fight was moved to December, and was again postponed, this time because of the poor weather. The fight had to be moved indoors or postponed until the warmer weather set in.

We finally got the indoor fight in January, 1944, with two guys who were supposed to be what is commonly called 'professional opponents', or, to put it simply, to give us a workout so we could get some much needed rounds in before a major fight. While I believe that they weren't instructed to lose, they weren't expected to win either, which they're losing records indicated. Our opponents were survivors who would just go out there and give us the work that we needed.

But the guys we fought were somewhat more than just survivors, as both of them could take a good punch and make us (or anyone they fought) look bad, and they were essentially experienced 10-round fighters. They gave us the work, even though they held on a lot and knew how to slip punches.

Billy finally won his first decision, but that was because the guy he was fighting knew all the tricks on how to hold on and survive. Even with that, he still had to hold on to be saved by the bell, in the final round. I also won a much easier decision. And we both got our ten rounds of work in that Paulie said we both needed.

I don't know if they do it now-a-days, but in those days, they wanted you to eat a lot of fish and pasta before a fight, or at least Paulie insisted on it. He said "that carbohydrates would give you the extra energy you need to go the distance. And eating meat before a fight would only give you bad cramps if you took a hard shot to the stomach."

I hope that someday I'll get the chance to speak to some of these new trainers and find out if they still use this diet and why they seem to refuse to teach defense anymore. I also wonder what types of training methods they do use today, that they didn't use in my day. The fighters are much bigger and stronger today. My gut feeling is that fighters are bulking up on steroids, which is going to be very dangerous to the boxers, who don't need more risks involved with our sport.

I'd also ask the trainers if they still preach sexual abstinence two - six weeks before a fight. What type of food do they want you to eat before a bout? How much roadwork must a fighter do? Remember we fought often and it was 15 rounds in those days, not 12 rounds like today for a title bout.

Sure, I still do get invited to a lot of functions, to mingle with fight fans and old friends, and sometimes sign autographs, and I'd be lying if I said I didn't enjoy that. It's great to be remembered by the fan. Mingling with old opponents certainly brings back memories as well.. I've never been inducted or even nominated to the Hall of Fame, and while it would be a great honor, it would be my kids who would be around far longer. who would enjoy it, should it ever happen.

But my health has deteriorated greatly, as I grow older, and I only have my mind left. I'm lucky to still have my mind, considering the amount of punches I have taken. The great love of my life, is Jodie, whom I know I can truly rely on. The reflexes are long since gone.

I would imagine that with all the sanctioning bodies that are around today, Billy and I could have won a lot of championship belts. These fighters today, they only have to fight 15 fights or so to become a so called champion. In our day, some of us would fight 15 times in a year, or even more.

And, all these weight divisions, and 12-round title fights. I just don't understand it. I think Paulie and Uncle Johnny would be turning over in their graves if they saw what boxing has now become. Fifteen rounds have always been the true test of a world champion and there should only be only one sanctioning body and eight weight classes, nine at the most.

As for clowns like Mike Tyson, well every generation has its share of oddballs, and in truth, so does every sport, It's just not publicized as much.

Sure, the more weight divisions and the more sanctioning bodies we have, the more titles are around for the kids to win. And that knowledge gives them extra incentive and does get them off the streets and into the gyms. And if they train properly, away from the evils of drugs as well.

But as for me, I really long for the old days, with just one sanctioning body and the eight or nine weight divisions, and fifteen round fights, which to my mind is the real test of a true world champion. It takes a lot of dedication and hard work to train for those extra three championship rounds, and it also builds character. This is something that seems to be badly missing in boxing today.

But the fact is that Billy and I also fought during the war years, a time when a lot of the fighters or potential fighters went off to serve our country. Some of them could have probably been world champions. But the shortage of competition also limited the amounts of fights we had. And the competition we faced probably would have been a lot tougher, had it not been for WWII. A lot of the brave Americans serving their Country. They risked and many lost their careers and worse their lives, but that is the way it was and the way it should have been. One of my few regrets is that I wasn't among them.

Chapter V

It was July, 1945. The war in Europe was finally over and the victory celebrations were going on throughout our great nation. The Nazi madman who had led Germany to its destruction had committed suicide in his bunker, although we didn't know it at the time. However what we did know for sure that the Nazis had finally given up, although not without a long and very bloody fight.

The Russians had taken East Germany and the rest of the Allied forces controlled the Western part of the Country. The Capital of Berlin was also divided into East and West sectors.

Early in August, an atomic bomb would be dropped on Nagasaki and Hiroshima, Japan, creating unbelievable destruction, injuries and death, and the war in the Pacific would soon be over as well.

It was a darn shame that mom and Uncle Johnny didn't live long enough to see the victory. It would have gladdened their hearts. Mom had passed away a year earlier when we gave our family doctor who was taking care of her, the okay to pull the plug. It was against our religious beliefs, but the doctor gave us the choice, and we didn't want mom to suffer any longer.

Uncle Johnny had a massive heart attack and passed away just before the armistice on the battleship Missouri was signed off the coast of Japan. So our two guiding lights had passed away the same year, leaving Billy and I to take care of each other, which, because of our upbringing was fairly easy to do.

Neither mom or Uncle Johnny really had ever learned the truth, that much of their families who had been living in Eastern Europe were taken by rail to various concentration camps in Poland and Austria, and, like so many other innocent, non-Aryan people, had perished in the Nazi death camps. I never heard from any of our overseas relatives before or since.

Sadly, our brave leader throughout most of the war, also never lived to see the end of it. President Franklin Delano Roosevelt had a massive stroke and died in Warm Springs Georgia. It was now going to be up to Vice President Harry Simpson Truman, to take over and see to the final ending of the Second World War. He would make the fatal decision to end the war with Japan with the dropping of the Atomic Bomb. It wasn't pretty. Almost everyone in America agreed that it was a necessary move to bring the war to a quick end, and thereby save many American lives.

So at this moment in time, Japan was just those two huge atomic bomb mushroom cloud blasts away from surrendering, but obviously we didn't know it then. In fact, we didn't have any concept of what the damage the Atomic Bomb could actually do. It was a well kept secret. We also had no knowledge of the horror of seeing innocent Japanese citizens pay the ultimate price for a war they may not have really wanted to fight, or believed in. Hell, it was rough for us here in America to watch the devastation.

But the Japanese were then using their planes as bombs, crash into our ships, committing suicide in the hopes that they would destroy our Navy. They were called Kamikaze pilots, but we just called them fucking nuts! Of course they did damage many ships and kill many American seamen, but never came close to accomplishing their hoped for result of keeping the Allied forces away.

No one could ever foresee that the Kamikazes were the start of an idea that ultimately lead to the terrorists attack and destruction of the Twin Towers of the World Trade Center in New York City, on Sept. 11, 2001.

So now, except for Aunt Jen, who kept to herself even more since the passing of Uncle Johnny, and Paulie, who seemed to be always by our side, Billy and I were now totally alone and on our own. We had no more family that we knew of in the States. But we did have the confidence that life experience as well as boxing had given us, and enough money to live comfortably, thanks to our boxing skills. But all that didn't give us the someone special we needed to talk to when the times warranted it.

I think that it was much easier for Billy, who had quietly married his girlfriend Mary, in a civil ceremony shortly after mom's passing, and the three of us were now living together in mom's apartment, with Billy and Mary taking the larger bedroom.

The good news was that Mary was a great cook and if I wasn't careful, I probably could have easily become a heavyweight. But Billy never spoke about Mary very much in front of mom. She wanted Billy to marry into the Greek Orthodox Church and Mary was very much a Protestant. Rather than risking to upset mom, Billy waited till she passed away before he got married.

I met Mary on a number of occasions and we even double dated at times, catching a movie together at the local cinema. I liked Mary. She was kind of goofy, always full of laughs and seemed to really enjoy life, although on more than one occasion she expressed to me her dislike of boxing.

I guess it was much harder for me to adjust to mom and Johnny's passing than Billy. Sure, the memories of both were always around us, but, except for their illness, and the poor condition they were in when they passed away, we had good memories. At least by getting married, Billy always had someone to talk to, while I was getting somewhat lonely.

At that particular point in my life, I really felt like I needed someone to be with, or at least have something that was tangible around me to hold on to. Something or someone I could grasp and say, 'this is mine'.

It wasn't as if I didn't like girls, I certainly did, and had my share of enjoyable sexual relations at times, but my entire focus in life at that time was aimed at becoming someone special, a world middleweight champion. And I knew I needed someone special by my side to share the fruits of my labor.

There again is where boxing came into play. Winning the middleweight title now had even more meaning to me, and I wanted that belt and the money and recognition that came with it, more than anything in the world. Not just for me, but for mom and Uncle Johnny, who I knew were both in Heaven, watching over us. Billy and I intended to win the titles and make them proud and we both knew how proud they would be.

To be sure, there were always the groupies, the hangers on who wanted to be around a future champion. That is what has become the entourage of today. I had many opportunities to enjoy a very healthy sex life. I did, but if I wanted more, it was always available.

But boxing was my biggest priority and I was determined to keep the promise I had made to mom and stay as celibate as possible until I found the right gal and got married. It wasn't that hard as the groupies always followed Billy around more than me, because he was a bigger puncher as well as much better looking. And they didn't seem to care if he was married or not. To his credit, I don't think Billy ever took advantage of these opportunities and always remained faithful to Mary, although it was never discussed.

Still, I was feeling very frustrated at this point of my life, and Paulie had to continually caution me not to work as hard as I was, because, as he would put it, 'I could easily leave the fight as well as the upcoming title shot in the gym'. Paulie wanted me to be as sharp as possible for that big match that had been scheduled for August 10.

Billy also had trained very hard, but he was spending a lot more time at home with his wife Mary, and did not seem to be as determined as I was, although he was also going to fight for the welterweight title on the same August card. I think it was because he knew how much power he had in that big right-hand of his.

But as I now recall, thinking that Billy was easing up may be have been nothing more than my loneliness speaking out. We still were very close, as we lived together, but it wasn't like it was before he got married. We certainly always did our roadwork and the required exercises in the gym, including the jump rope, the shadow boxing and hard sparring. But it just didn't seem the same. Something was missing.

In fact, Paulie had upped Billy's roadwork to four-five miles a day until a week before the big fight. I thought it was a bit strange that he never asked me to run more. I just figured that he knew that I always ran with Billy anyway. Paulie obviously knew that neither of us had fought 15 round fights before and we had to be in extra good condition just in case we had to go the distance.

The double title fight-card was held at the Philadelphia Coliseum on August 10 1945. And while Billy remained undefeated, with nothing but KO's on his record, I still had that one loss, early in my career, as the only black mark, as well as the one draw. Both with Bob Harrison, who unfortunately was forced to retire from the fight game with a heart problem, and was now working in a munitions plant to support our war effort.

But Bob kept dropping by the gym to give Billy and me encouragement. Boxing is one of those sports that respect alone can make friends out of staunch enemies. You earn that respect just by getting in the ring and being willing to compete one on one.

Although Harrison, was now supporting his family by working in a defense plant, he always made sure that a week before our big fight, he stopped by the gym again to wish Billy and myself good luck. The guy may have been a somewhat dirty fighter as a pro, but he was a class act outside of the ring. Bob promised that he'd be at ringside with his wife, rooting for both of us, and he proved to be true to his word.

The Coliseum appeared to be packed to the rafters, and the blue-gray smoke hung high overhead like a cloud. The crowd noise was deafening, as we entered the arena and slowly walked to our dressing room, which like just about everything else at the time, we had to share. In fact, as often as not, we had to share it with other fighters, but it was not the case this night.

139

Paulie appeared to have us both very sharp and at the top of our game. He in fact cut back almost all of the sparring and roadwork the final week of training to avoid having us over-train and leave our fights in the gym. He had never trained a World Champion before, and he wanted to have at least one of us change that.

The contract called for the 15-round championship distance fights, with both Billy and I guaranteed $20,000 apiece. Not much money today, but more than enough money to buy ourselves a new home and car in those post-war days.

I knew that if Billy won, he and Mary, and the baby that was now on the way, would probably leave me for much larger living accommodations. I would remain living at moms. I guess it was a bit selfish on my part to think that way, and while I never mentioned it to Billy, I was almost hoping that he would lose or get a draw, so our family would remain together.

Of course that feeling changed to pride the moment that he started his walk down the long dark aisle to contest the world welterweight title. Paulie was walking down the aisle beside him, along with a top cut man that he had hired for this fight. Since Billy never cut, I didn't know if this was needed, but I had always trusted Paulie's judgment.

I had to remain in the dressing room to continue to loosen up, but I did have a small radio to listen to the fight while I continued to shadowbox and work up a nice sweat, in front of a large full-length mirror.

The welterweight champion at the time was Delroy Brown, a fast, converted southpaw, who had far more ring experience than Billy. Billy, unfortunately I felt, never had faced a left-hander, who could switch to fighting with the other hand at the drop of a hat. He worked with a few southpaws in the gym, but didn't look very good doing it. I had fought lefties before, and I knew that this could be a very difficult style for Billy to deal with. I had warned him in advance, but he told me that Paulie prepared him for that style, so I let it drop.

I also realized then that this was why Paulie had hired a top cut man, since accidental head butts were not uncommon when a southpaw fought a conventional right handed fighter. He didn't want to lose this fight on a bad cut. After all, it was the most important fight of either of both of our lives.

Paulie was a pretty fair fighter in his day, but as a trainer, he was not highly thought of, and he wanted that to change. Hell, he was a good guy and deserved some credit.

So, although Paulie explained the problem of fighting against this style, and he kept showing Billy which way to move, and how to plant his feet and keep away from Delroy's power, I wasn't sure that Billy had absorbed all of it. Billy did have a lot on his mind at this time. He needed the money very badly, for his growing family, and just wanted to go out there and get another fast knockout. It was not a fast knockout.

Brown, a tall, slender black guy, was a real cutey, who had a good sense of what he had to do in the ring at all times. He probably needed a trainer as much as he needed to enter the ring drunk. He knew full well what he had to do, and I really believed that his corner crew was only there for show.

Brown was, like Billy and I, from Pennsylvania, but he was based in the Pittsburgh area in the Western part of the State. And he also had brought a fairly large contingent of fans with him for the big fight. The Pittsburgh vs. Philadelphia battles always drew large crowds. And in those days before Pay-Per-View, these large crowds where a promoter's dream.

Billy had a few pounds in weight, the power and youth in his favor.

Brown had all that ring experience going for him, as well as a small reach advantage and the ability to bang with either hand. Although he didn't have a lot of knockouts, Delroy knew how to wear down his opponents and instinctively knew when they were hurt. Most important, he had the killer instinct to finish his opponent off when he felt that he had him softened up enough.

Billy wore a newly made gold hooded robe and wore his customary gold and green trunks with the blue and white flag of Greece sewed onto them. Brown wore white trunks with a black stripe down both sides. He didn't wear a robe as he entered the ring.

As they walked down the aisle to the frenzied cheers of the crowd, it was hard to tell whom they favored. Even the radio announcer wasn't able to make that call with any certainty. I continued to shadowbox in front of the tall mirror, and listened to the guy on the radio call the blow by blow action. This announcer was very good, and really made you feel like you were sitting at ringside, watching the fight.

Finally, the referee gave the fighters their final instructions, at center ring. The fighters touched gloves and the battle for the welterweight title, as well as the mythical battle for the Pennsylvania State Crown had begun.

My assessment of Billy having trouble handling Brown's style proved all too accurate. The announcer said that by round six, 'Brown appeared to be well ahead on points'. I wished that I could have been there, at ringside, telling Billy to circle and look for the opening, but I knew in my heart that Paulie was telling him all that and much more.

Still I had this feeling of absolute helplessness in the pit of my stomach that I never liked. My brother Billy was in danger of losing his first fight and a chance at the world title. I was just nervously sitting and then pacing in the dressing room doing nothing but waiting and occasionally taking a big swing at the heavy bag to rid myself of the frustrations.

Round seven was going pretty much the same way as the previous six rounds, with Brown constantly flicking the left jab in Billy's face and piling up points while continuing to frustrate my brother, who had that very short fuse to begin with. To add to all the problems, according to the announcer who was calling the fight on the radio, Billy appeared to be getting very tired and a 'small trickle of blood was coming from his nose'.

'Darn it!' I thought. I was right. He had needed more work. He should have listened to me and have waited to get married. I turned and pounded away at the heavy bag, again in frustration. 'Billy had just not taken this fight seriously enough' I thought.

In a flash Billy proceeded to prove me wrong. 'A fast left-right combination stuns the champion, and Petrovic now has him against the ropes, whaling away at his face and body'. The radio blared, "Brown's trying to cover up, but it's not working, punches are getting through!. A right to Brown's head, now a left, a couple of uppercuts, Brown is reeling. Blood is pouring from his nose and mouth. How much longer is his corner going to let this fight go on? Holy cow, what a turnaround. This fight should be stopped now! What's wrong with the ref? He's looking in but doing nothing."

I felt that a far better question would have been when was Billy going to unleash that big overhand right, always his Sunday punch. This punch had accounted for almost all of his career knockouts.

As if Billy had read my mind, "Petrovic lands an overhand right, Brown's knees are wobbly. Brown is down! The crowd is roaring! The referee is counting, one, two, three…Brown's not going to make it to his feet. The ref is waving it off. It's over! It's over! Billy Petrovic is the new welterweight champion of the world."

"Yes! Yes! Yes!" I yelled, pumping my arms skyward, in my empty dressing room. No one was around yet I was jumping up and down and raising my arms to the sky, thanking the Lord, as the ring announcer gave the time as; "At one minute twenty one seconds of the seventh round, the winner and *new* welterweight champion of the world, and the pride of South Philadelphia, Billy 'Mr. KO' Petrovic!"

I don't know where the announcer picked up Billy's new 'Mr. KO' nickname. Neither of us had heard it used before, he may have just made it up, but we both liked it. It fit Billy to a tee.

The noise was deafening as Paulie returned to the dressing room first, a huge grin on his face, followed by Billy and his cut man. Paulie turned and instructed the police officer who was guarding the dressing room door that there will be no one else allowed until after the main event. The press would just have to wait.

Mary was not on hand, as we feared that if a problem arose during the fight, it could endanger her pregnancy. Paulie felt it was always very bad luck to have a pregnant woman at ringside. Besides, Mary really didn't like the sport very much, anyway.

We all hugged. Billy, who for what may have been the first time in his adult life, was actually crying. Tears were flowing from both his eyes. "This one's for you Mom, Mary, Uncle Johnny," he yelled, looking towards Heaven and turning to me, "Now it's your turn, Tony", bring home the belt and the champagne will flow for a week."

I rarely drank and hated champagne and I didn't have a lot of time to take in the full meaning of Billy's words. A police officer knocked gently on the dressing room door, as I replied, "How about it flowing forever?" Billy didn't respond as the guard at the door hollered, you're on, Tony".

Paulie quickly finished wrapping my hands tightly and slid the gloves on.

I felt like a million bucks walking down the aisle, to the roar of the crowd. I was wearing my lucky gold boxing shorts, with a newly made gold robe, also adorning a sewn on Greek flag, courtesy of Billy's wife, Mary. She wasn't Greek, but certainly respected our beliefs. Little did I know that the blood that would be pouring off the heads of both me and my opponent. would soon badly stain these lucky shorts crimson.

Still, it was quite a load off my mind to know the reputation of the Petrovic Brothers wasn't going to rest entirely on my shoulders for this fight. My little brother Billy had taken care of that, and right now, he stood ten feet tall in my eyes. I was very proud of him. Now I was able to relax a bit, or should have been able to, had I not been hyperventilating.

I thought I had calmed down completely by the time I reached the ring, but Paulie threw a small, cold towel at me, and when he wiped my head, I was full of sweat. All this excitement gave me a new feeling, one that I liked. I liked it a lot. It was a feeling I still remember till this day.

I sat down on the stool, pretending to listen to Paulie's last minute instructions, but if I heard him, I sure don't remember anything that he said to me. I was ready to go now. All I could visualize in my mind was the image of Billy and I standing at center ring displaying our newly won belts, together.

Then it was back to reality as the ref called my opponent, the champion, and myself to ring center.

My opponent, the then middleweight champion was William 'Dutch' Schultz, a newly crowned champion, since he had won the title in his previous fight.

Because of the recent world war and his obvious Aryan looks and heritage, the noisy crowd was to be entirely in my corner.

Schultz had a short, razor top military haircut, with blonde hair and blue eyes. He looked like a real Aryan. He seemed a bit bigger than me, and was heavily muscled with a tattoo of "Mother" on a red heart, on his right muscle. He had another tattoo on his left, but I can't recall what it was. We had a long stare-down as the ref gave his instructions and we touched gloves.

The fight wouldn't have even lasted a round, if I had hated this Aryan the way the crowd obviously did. But how could I hate him? Even if I wanted to, I knew that Billy had taken our family to glory, and right now I couldn't be mad at anyone. Besides, just because he was obviously of German heritage didn't make him a bad guy. The fact that he was the world champion also gave me cause for respect.

The bell rang, and Schultz used his superior upper body strength to bully me across the ring. He had me in his corner pounding away, at my body, while I was in a semi-crouch, covering up my face and chin and returning punches when I was able to, which wasn't very often. "Turn him around" I heard someone I thought was Paulie shout. But Schultz was far too strong for that. I saw an opportunity to land a solid uppercut to his chin, but as my head came up, it made contact with his, and suddenly the ring was bright red, stained with our blood, and I sure had gotten one heck of a headache. I only had to blink to know I had been badly cut.

At our present time, this fight would have been stopped at once, and called a technical draw.

But this was 1945, and the only way a fight would be stopped was by the corner throwing in the towel or on rare occasion by the referee, if he didn't' think that you were fighting back enough.

We touched gloves in apology, and as I tried to focus. I could see that he was cut above his left eye, a deep gash. I was also cut on my scalp, over my right eye, and the blood was pouring down, along with the sweat, dripping into and burning both my eyes. The canvas and everything around me was quickly turning a bright shade of crimson.

The crowd, who was obviously in my corner, was yelling at the ref to disqualify Schultz", but I suspect that they really knew that it was an accidental head butt, and he was no more at fault than I was, probably even less.

We finished the round, mainly be staying away from each other, so we could get to our corners and allow our cut men to do their job.

The ref came over to visit both our corners between rounds to ask if we were okay. I doubt either of us was. The blood from my scalp, and the burning of the solution used to close the wound, didn't help my pounding head. I didn't drink then, but since I retired I do now, on rare occasion, and this pounding in my temples was far worse than any hangover that I ever had.

Round two, saw far less blood but also much less action. We both pretty well just jabbed at each other in center-ring, looking for an opportunity to work the cuts and seize the advantage that we both now fully realized would eventually decide the holder of world title belt.

By round three Schultz had an egg-sized lump over his left eye, and Paulie made sure he mentioned that "it's an inviting target". Open it up, and his corner will have no choice, but to throw in the towel, because he won't be able to see. As it is, he's wide open for your right hand. He won't see it coming. Don't worry about your cut, you'll be fine. End the fight this round".

It was very easy for him to say, as the blood was still rapidly pouring into my eyes, and I could hardly see. To add to my misery, I was literally seeing red and had this terrific headache. All I wanted to do was see the fight end, one way or the other and take a dozen or so aspirins.

So when we came out for round three, I think we both realized that one way or the other, this was going to be our final round of the night. I followed

Paulie's advice, circling Schultz to the right so he'd have a difficult time following me with his very limited vision. Suddenly I saw the opening and lunged at him, throwing one of the strongest right hands I can ever remember delivering. It landed flush on the lump over Schultz's eye, opening it up again and splattering blood everywhere, including all over my already blurred eye. Now it was obvious that Schultz could no longer see.

The crowd went wild. This time his corner immediately threw in the towel, and the ref waved it off, and suddenly the Petrovic Brothers were both world champions. But I just wasn't in shape to get very emotional. All I wanted was aspirins and some sleep.

When Schultz and I embraced in his corner, he asked me for a rematch, and under the circumstances I told him 'absolutely'. Paulie wasn't very happy that I was speaking for him, but he was so caught up in the moment that he probably would have authorized a rematch that same night, cut and all. He never had a world champion before and all of a sudden he had two in one evening.

The dressing room was packed to the gills. We quickly pushed our way into it, and Billy was the first one to greet me with a big bear hug. Then he noticed the cut, which he had to have heard about on the radio. He said 'looks like you'll be needing a few stitches, Tony'. I was sure that was true but I wanted to try to savor every minute of this night, right then, and if I lost a little blood, no big deal. "Yeah, but so will Dutch", I responded, "but first I need a couple of aspirins."

The head kept pounding while the press began to ask their questions, Paulie informed them that there indeed would be a rematch, if Schultz really wanted it. He doubted that he would. He was glaring at me, obviously annoyed that I had made the commitment already, while he made the statement to the press.

After about 15 minutes of non-stop questions and answers, Paulie ushered the press out of the way, and let Billy answer the rest of the questions so I could take a shower and grab a cab to the hospital. I got seven stitches just above my hairline. Billy stayed around to answer all the questions they had of him, then grabbed a cab to meet us at the hospital.

In the cab that Paulile and I took to the hospital, he kept berating me for trying to be my own manager and booking my own fights. I told him I was just trying to be a good sport. The fight should never have ended the way that it did, because the head butt was really my fault. Paulie agreed, but still said "I brought you to the title. From now on, I'll match all of your fights or you'll find yourself without a manager. Remember I'm also your promoter." He was right and I didn't have reason to argue. "And", Paulie continued, I better teach you the correct way to turn your opponent around before you fight that guy again."

We all returned home very late, but Billy, Mary and Aunt Jen, along with Paulie and a number of our neighbors had set up a big block party for us. A local Italian deli provided the food and drinks, and an accordion provided most of the music. Billy and Mary provided some pretty good dancing. She could really move for a gal five months pregnant.

I was never very good at hoofing it, and since I didn't have a girl friend at the time, there really was no need for me to learn how to dance. So I just leaned back against a black sedan, and took in the goings on. Besides, I had an ice bag on my head because the headache had not yet deserted me.

"Enjoy it, you guys really earned it tonight," I heard a soft, sweet feminine voice with a very noticeable southern accent. I turned to find a beautiful gal who would come to be the girl of my dreams. Her name was Jodie Darwin, and she was dressed in a white, polka-dot dress and had a big blue ribbon in her long blonde, wavy hair. Her father John was an ex heavyweight contender, so Jodie really knew the sport inside out. "Want to dance, champ?"

Without giving me a chance to respond in the negative, she grabbed me, put the ice bag on the car, took me around the waist and obviously figuring out quickly that I was pretty awkward on the dance floor, whispered in my ear "just follow my lead, Tony. You'll do just fine".

I remembered Jodie from high school, she was in one of my classes, but I never gave her (or anyone else then) the time of day. Jodie had filled out a lot since those days. She was wearing a light sweater, and looked like some Greek Goddess. I smiled at her, and she returned it in kind as the band played on.

Jodie had indeed grown a lot since our high school days and now looking at her, I thought she could easily be the next Miss America. She was totally gorgeous. Love at second sight? Perhaps, but this was way to smooth for me. I thought I was dreaming.

I didn't know it at the time, but this night, Aug. 10, 1945, was going to be one of the happiest nights of my life, and not just from the two boxing victories and world title belts that Billy and I achieved.

Paulie decided to give us some much-needed time off, to enjoy our new celebrity status and give me some extra time for the battle scars to heal. He also gave us two envelopes with checks totaling about $40,000, less taxes and his percentage. It was now time for the Petrovic's to find a new home.

Now that I had met Jodie, and started going out with her, although only for a few months, I really didn't want to move away from her. I was with her constantly. She made me laugh and sometimes made me laugh so hard, I cried. She was living just a block away from mom's house. I thought about letting Billy and Mary move, and Jodie and I would remain in our house.

Billy understood my feelings. Nothing really needed to be said, but, after a brief conversation, Billy convinced me that we should buy a duplex together, in a good neighborhood and I would ask Jodie to marry and move in with me. They'd take the bottom floor since they had a baby on the way and it was hard for Mary to climb stairs, and we'd take the upstairs apartment.

It really wasn't a very tough decision for me. I had fallen deeply in love with Jodie, but I still didn't know for sure how she felt about me. I suppose that I was just too shy to ask. Jodie had always told me that "I was very special to her" and that was about it. Maybe, for the first time in my life, I felt a bit reserved. I suppose that's why I wasn't that much more vocal than she was about my feelings towards her..

Jodie and I had become inseparable, so on a beautiful moonlit evening in late October, we were slowly walking home after a movie, holding hands, and I just got up the courage and told her how I felt and that I wanted to marry her and spend the rest of my life with her.

At first Jodie had a blank stare on her face, as if she had not been expecting this, but suddenly the tears came flowing down her cheeks, and a smile came to her lips. "I'm so happy! Of course I'll marry you, Tony."

The first problem came when I told her that I wanted to elope or at least to get married quickly, so we could buy the duplex. Our soldiers were still returning home from the war, getting married and buying up a lot of the choice property.

That's when Jodie hesitated. "Quickly? How quickly?"

"How about tomorrow? Does that work for you?" I impulsively replied. "Otherwise, tonight will work for me!"

"That's a bit too quick for me, Tony. Let's wait until we can have a real big wedding", she said.

I thought I would have to change my plans with Billy if we waited too long, so I told Jodie that I needed to speak to him first, as he was my only living family. Okay, Aunt Jen was also family but she never interfered in anything Billy and I wanted to do.

Billy smiled broadly when I told him. "Great! Congratulations!" He mussed my hair. "We'll just buy the house now, and you and Jodie move in after you get married, or earlier if you want and Jodie can join you after you get married. The upstairs will remain vacant till then, although we could move in the furniture whenever you want to. It's your call, Tony."

It was a very simple solution. So why didn't I think of it? I did know Jodie wanted to remain chaste until after marriage, and I while I had very strong feelings about her sexually, I knew I loved her too much not to accept her wishes. So except for some occasional heavy petting Jodie remained a virgin until we married.

Jodie, who had a fairly large family, agreed with our decision, and the housing problem was resolved.

There was one other major problem that we hadn't counted on, our religions. I was Greek Orthodox and she was Roman Catholic. At first it seemed like it was obviously going to be a big problem. The problem wasn't so much for us, because we had nobody left we had to please, but for her family. Neither of us wanted to convert, but if it had to happen, I told Jodie that I would do it. Except for Aunt Jen, there was nobody close to me who would get upset about it. And as I said, she never interfered. Besides, that way Jodie could keep her family happy.

That potential problem too was quickly solved, as we decided to simply have a smaller wedding, done by a Justice of the Peace. If her family could handle that, we could always have a bigger wedding later or a huge celebration in a big hall. It was all Billy's idea, as he and Mary had also been married by a Justice of the Peace.

So on a snowy New Years Day, 1946, Jodie and I were married by the Justice of the Peace in Philadelphia City Hall. Billy was a witness as was Jodie's mom. Then it was time to move into the new house that Billy had brought and start a life together with Jodie. Mary had given birth to Billy

Jr., a beautiful 7'6" ounce boy. So the Petrovic family was growing again. Maybe, just maybe Billy Jr. would become a future boxing champion as well.

Jodie and I never had that big wedding, but we did have a huge reception in a large Italian restaurant, band and all which Mary and Billy had rented for us for the day. They said it was their wedding present to us, and it was much appreciated.

Chapter VI

1946, marked the first session of the newly formed United Nations in New York City. It also brought into the open the horrific acts of Nazi Germany in the concentration camps, with the Nuremberg Trials, and the hanging of most of the leaders of the mass exterminations of Jews and Gypsies, probably including much of our family. The vivid images of the death camps still linger in my mind.

And in boxing, former world heavyweight champion Jack Johnson was killed in a car accident in North Carolina.

But for Billy and I, it was to be business as usual. After the wedding and reception, Billy and I immediately went back into serious training for our next title defenses. It didn't seem right not being able to have a honeymoon, but everyone knew that it would come in the future, when time and money was not to be a factor.

We were training for what was to be an exact rematch, bout wise, of our first title fight card, since almost everybody thought that Delroy Smith would have beaten Billy if he had just been able to stay away from his power.

Maybe Smith could have won the decision, but staying away from a fast, big puncher like my brother, for fifteen rounds, was never an easy task, even for a slick, jab and move fighter like Delroy Smith.

I didn't realize it till many years later, because Billy had never told anyone, (it was one of the few things he kept from me) but he had begun getting many life threatening letters and calls for fighting against a black fighter, who never had the same opportunity in any sport that the white man did, back then. But boxing was the one sport that was in the forefront of racial equality in sports, and rightly so.

Racism was still part of America's legacy, and many white Southerners were continuing to fight the Civil War, and hoping that 'the South would indeed rise again.' The Klu Klux Clan was still going strong, preaching their hatred. Although I don't recall any of the neo-Nazi skinheads being around back then. I guess hate has been and always will be part of our world, although I believe it's more a statement of jealousy of those who have not, against those who have.

The only reason I was able to find out about the threats, was through all of the hate mail and notes that Billy had kept well hidden, so Mary wouldn't find out and cause him further grief in furthering his boxing career.

It was strange, that I fought Bob Harrison a couple of times but never received any threats. But the truth is, I never had any threats.. The reason may have been that these fights were held in "The City of Brotherly Love", and not South of the Mason Dixon Line.

Neither Billy nor I ever learned or understood prejudice at our home or in school. We knew that it was going on in the South, and that blacks were treated as second class citizens, via Jim Crow laws, but we never fully realized the full extent of it, until Billy decided to take a fight in Charleston, South Carolina.

I know that if Mary would have found out about the letters, Billy probably would have been forced to stop boxing and change professions, and he might still be alive today. Hindsight is always 20-20. Billy, like myself, never had any use for prejudice. To us it was plain stupidity. It didn't belong in life or in any sport, and certainly not in boxing, where everyone was equal when the bell rings.

Mom and Uncle Johnny had brought us up to respect everyone, and that's exactly what we did. Hate was a four-letter word that should only have been found in the dictionary, if that, and not in our everyday vocabulary. Besides, how could you not respect anyone who had the courage to step into the ring with you and slug it out, one on one? That courage alone deserves an enormous amount of respect. And every boxer we had fought we respected and I assume vice-versa.

Sure, we would always read about how bad the blacks were being treated down South, having to use separate toilets, water fountains, and eat in segregated restaurants. We knew that as stupid as it was, the fact that blacks had to ride in the back of busses existed in the south. But reading about it and seeing it first hand were two different things.

We also realized that blacks weren't able to get the type of quality education that a white man could. There seemed to be very little that we could do to improve their lot in life, which would finally start to improve during the Kennedy administration. The use of 'affirmative action' was also helpful, although I'm not sure we still need that today. We did, make open statements to the press that we completely supported all those brave folks who were fighting for the rights of the black folks in the South. We had even discussed the possibility of becoming 'freedom marchers' and help lead the fight for equality.

It was a very sad time in our history. These mistreated minorities in the Southern States didn't really ask for much, mainly equality. They wanted to be treated exactly like any other human being. And why not? They are no different than anyone else.

I remember once stopping by a restaurant in Southern Maryland when I was younger. I can't remember much of the details, but I can vividly recall a sign on the door of the establishment, it read 'No colored or dogs allowed'. This was the lot of many blacks living in the South in the mid 20th century, and slavery had already been dead more than 100 years, at least legally. Talk about man's inhumanity to man.

I was going to fight Bill Schultz again. I figured I owed him the rematch due to the head-butt, which I knew that I had caused, although it was not intentional on my part. A fight should be won or lost legally. And I had fouled Schultz, that much I knew.

Fortunately, the real fight fans also raised a bit of an uproar in favor of the rematch, so despite Paulie's initial objections that Schultz was still much too strong for me, the money was right and he allowed the fight to go on.

I thought it was a bit odd that Paulie was not having me do much roadwork or shadow boxing for the rematch, even though he at first told me that Schultz was too big and strong for me.

And he never showed me how to turn Bill Schultz around, as he had promised to, after our first fight. When I asked him about it, he just said "Ya don't have to knock yourself out, Tony, I was wrong. I really think that it's gonna be a very easy fight for ya. Ya really learned a lot in your first fight with Schultz." Strange, I thought, Paulie always had me working hard no matter how easy the opponent was supposed to be. At first he didn't even want me to take this fight. I figured that maybe the word was out that Schultz was going into the tank, and I didn't have to do much to win. I wanted to be wrong, and I was. Boy was I wrong.

But for now who was I to argue? Paulie was the boss and had been around the boxing business long before I was born. He knew which end was up and he had always made sure Billy and I had been well taken care of.

This double championship fight card took place on February 11, 1946, and once again at the Philadelphia Coliseum. I didn't think it was possible to get more attendance at this fight, as there was a major snowstorm blowing and powerful, freezing gusts of wind which would surely would prevent even the most diehard fight fans from coming out.

But fight fans again proved to be a hearty breed, and if there was an empty seat in the house, neither Billy nor I could see it.

After a few quick prelims, there was a loud knock on the dressing room door. "Tony, you're up next."

This was very odd. I thought I was supposed to be fighting the main event, I always had before. Then I thought that maybe Billy's fight must have fallen out. I looked at Paulie for some insight. He had a surprised look on his face but could only shrug his shoulders. "Ya know as much as I do. They musta figured they'll save the bigger puncher for the main event. You know how excited fans get about seein' the knockout. I guess they decided to put ya on first, Tony".

I didn't even have my hands wrapped yet, and I hadn't come close to have broken a sweat. Even the trainers of today will always tell you that you never should go into a fight 'cold' or 'dry'.

As Paulie was quickly wrapping my hands Billy told the security guard at the door that we needed about five more minutes. The realization then suddenly occurred to me, Paulie didn't really want me to win this fight. He had either made a bet on my opponent or was back in with the mob, maybe both. That would certainly explain why I went from a 2-1 betting favorite to . a 5-2 underdog on fight day. That was the information (the odds) that was reported in the local paper that morning.

I suddenly had this urge to shove Paulie's unlit cigar down his grizzled throat. But instead I figured out that we still needed him, and besides, Billy was up next. I kept my rage inside, knowing that poor Bill Schultz, like our last fight, was going to get the worst of it. I took a deep breath to try to relax. I knew that I didn't even have to work up a sweat to have the hatred and energy to destroy Schultz and teach Paulie a lesson he'd never forget. Nothing was going to stop me! Nothing!

Paulie quickly finished wrapping my hands with adhesive tape, and lacing up the gloves, adding the white tape to keep them secure to my wrists. Billy walked over and patted my butt to wish me luck, and I called him aside and whispered to him what my suspicions were. Then I said, "luck? I don't need luck! Schultz does. If I'm right, I need a quick knockout and Billy, I'm going to get one tonight!"

"No fuckin way! I don't believe it!" Billy shouted, loud enough for everyone in the dressing room, including Paulie to hear. Hell, it was probably loud enough for Schultz in the next dressing room to overhear. He glared at Paulie, shook his head, but said nothing to him.

"You have to trust me on this one, Billy" I said quietly. I'll explain after the fight. And believe me, I am going to make it a quick one. The way Paulie trained me, or rather didn't for this fight, I'm going to have to."

Paulie sensed that there was something different about the way I walked and spoke, (in truth I deliberately swaggered with confidence, which is something that I had never done before) down the aisle, a snarl instead of a smile upon my face. And I wasn't waving back to the fans, as I had become accustomed to doing in my previous fights.

I wasn't interested in anything more than taking all my frustrations out on my opponent, and I intended to give it my all from the first bell. I realized that I hadn't trained for 15 rounds and the only way I was going to win this fight was by a quick knockout. This was either going to be a very fast win for me, and Paulie was going to learn a lesson tonight, or I was going to get the ass kicking of my life, I thought.

"Are ya okay, Tony? Ya acting kinda funny," Paulie asked, over the roar of the large crowd. He probably noticed that my demeanor was a lot different than usual. I was hoping that he would see that.

"Never felt better in my entire life, Paulie. I'm ready for this fight, and I'm going to really kick some serious butt tonight. I'm going to take this guy out early. He'll never know what hit him. You really motivated me well, Paulie. I'm definitely up for this fight." I replied. Knowing that those words would probably upset him far more than anything else I could do or say at that moment.

And it must have done exactly that, because Paulie started to look at me strangely. He had never before seen me this confidant, I felt that he had to know or at least suspect that I was on to him. He reached up with his free hand and mopped his sweaty brow with his shirtsleeve. "Don't go for the early KO, Tony. That's a mistake. He's too strong. Just wear him down like I trained ya to".

I shook my head. "No Paulie, I feel way too good tonight. This fight is going to be very short and sweet".

Paulie responded with something. But I covered my ears indicating that because of the crowd noise I could not hear him. I knew that he was trying to talk me into fighting the fight his way, which could mean me losing and maybe even getting hurt, and that was not going to happen.

So despite the coolness of the arena, Paulie actually began to sweat all over, staining the armpit area of his shirt. It wasn't hot or humid in the arena, so I figured that my ideas about Paulie intending to double cross us had proved correct. I knew full well that he was no longer in my corner, and maybe was not going to be in Billy's either. And I knew that taking any advice from him at this point would be like asking him the easiest way on how to lose the fight and my title.

We reached the ring and I quickly ducked under the top strand of rope to get inside. I stepped into the box of resin that was always in the corners in those days to prevent a fighter from slipping. They don't use resin boxes today.

I had made up my mind as we walked down the aisle that this fight was going to be over in the first round. I decided that well before Paulie said 'Easy fight, Tony. Ya ready for him. Now, just take ya time and wear him down gradually. He got nuthin and ain't nothin' to worry about.'

I found it hard to believe that he was actually telling me all this bullshit with a straight face. He really sounded sincere. Still there was little doubt in my mind that Paulie had sold me out and maybe my kid brother as well. Even if I was wrong about Paulie, I knew that because of my insufficient training, I needed the early knockout.

We received the referee's instructions at center ring, staring each other down. We touched gloves and I went back to my corner, jumping up and down to try to work up a sweat. I really didn't want to waste any of my pent-up energy and I knew I was never that big a puncher. But I knew today that I had better have learned how to turn over a punch.

Schultz and I were both wearing what looked to be the same trunks that we wore in our first fight, minus the blood and sweat, of course.

The bell rang and we touched gloves again. As soon as we met in center ring I tore into Schultz like I never tore into anyone before, or since, in or out of the ring. I was throwing every punch I could, in every direction and angle possible, with his head being the main target.

I realize that there was some danger in giving Schultz an opening, but I figured there would be far more risk if I gave him the chance to recover and drag the fight on. I knew I hadn't trained for a long fight. Besides, I was never known as being a fast starter, and I hoped this tactic would surprise him. It did, and Paulie too.

Quickly I had muscled him back against the ropes, pounding away, and he had no way to escape the onslaught. I continued throwing punches from every angle. His legs suddenly seemed to be made of jelly, but why wasn't he going down? Maybe the ropes were holding him up. Why wasn't the referee jumping in between us and stopping the fight? Was he blind or did he also bet on Schultz?

I wanted this win badly, but I certainly didn't intend to kill my opponent. I kept thinking that the ref had to be in on the fix too? I yelled at the ref to stop the fight, but he just stood back and ignored me. If he was bought and paid for also, I was determined that like Paulie, he wasn't going to collect this bet.

I didn't take a lot of time to think about it. I turned over a solid overhand right, which landed flush on Schultz' temple and he went down like a rock hitting water. I think it was the hardest punch I had ever thrown and I knew immediately that he wasn't going to beat the count, and judging by the loud roar, the crowd knew it as well. It was all over at 1:16 of the first round.

In truth, with all the anger I had inside me at the time, I think the fight was over well before the first bell had rung.

I found out later that I had thrown more punches in 76 seconds than in any entire 3-minute round in my ring career.

The fight had ended, and the crowd was roaring so loud, I could hardly hear myself think. Then I noticed, while the referee was raising my hand in victory, Schultz was still lying flat on his back, his corner team and the fight doctor surrounding him. A stretcher and oxygen tank was called for and Schultz was taken to a nearby hospital by ambulance.

Billy was supposed to be the big puncher in the family, how on earth did this happen? I thought to myself. Where did all that power suddenly come from? It had to be the adrenaline. In truth Paulie helped me win this fight, more then he would ever know.

I turned to Paulie who seemed to be as red-faced as I had ever seen him, and immediately knew that my suspicions about him were correct.

I had wanted to knock Schultz out, but I had no intention of hurting him badly. I began to worry. 'What if I had killed him?' No win in the world would ever be worth having to live with that on my conscience for the rest of my life. Why was that damn piece of shit referee so slow in jumping in?

Not knowing if Schultz was going to make it or not took some of the edge off the win, I had wanted so badly.

And it came as no surprise that Paulie's negative attitude wasn't exactly what you'd call 'congratulatory'. "Nice work, Tony. But what da fuck were you doin' out there? I'm your trainer. Ya supposed to follow my instructions. I told you to take your time and wear him down. Look what you did to him. You mighta killed him. Whatsa matta, with ya, can't ya hear? What the fuck am I training ya for? Don't ya ever fuckin listen? They're taking Schultz out on a stretcher. I'm really disappointed in ya."

Paulie always talked fast and his East Coast slang could easily be picked up, especially when he was angry.

I was just about to tell Paulie that he was through talking and was fired, and to take a long walk on a short pier, but I has to hold back. I just couldn't do that with Billy's fight up next. I really think that if he wasn't so old I could have sent him into the balcony with one punch. But I couldn't leave my little brother without a manager or a corner.

And I wasn't going to make any move until I spoke to Billy. We always decided things together. I was just hoping that Paulie wasn't trying to get Billy to lose also, but figured that he wasn't because Billy had trained properly for his fight.

I admit the thought did cross my mind that if Paulie had lost some money on me, he could try to recoup his losses by betting against Billy. Then I figured that unless he had done so prior to the fight, he wouldn't have the time to do so now and he had trained Billy correctly.

The sound of a bell ringing brought me quickly back to reality.

"His corner should have thrown in the towel, or the ref should have had brains enough to stop the damn fight", I replied. "We all saw that I was kicking his ass, big time! It was a no-contest. Thanks Paulie, you really trained me well for this one."

I knew the words had stung him.

Billy was walking slowly down the aisle towards the ring, waving to the crowd, and I was walking the other way, towards the dressing room, also acknowledging the cheers.

When we passed each other, he had a big smile on his face. "Great fight, Tony", he said as we touched hands.

"Go get 'em, Billy, take him out early. We have a lot of celebrating to do", I yelled loud enough for Paulie to hear. Paulie turned and gave me a dirty look, but quickly and quietly left my side and walked back towards the ring with Billy.

I waited by the radio, anxiously waiting to listen to Billy's fight, before taking my shower. I had worked up a heavy sweat in a very short time, and really needed the shower, but I needed to hear all of Billy's fight.

Hopefully Paulie would have the decency to have him ready to win. And I also was awaiting news about Bill Schultz, who was now in the hospital. Besides, Delroy Smith was not known as a very big puncher.

And Billy had learned a lot from his first fight with Smith, and now with a child at home, he had that extra fire in the belly, the incentive that you often need to keep you going, the extra edge given by motivation.

Of course he too felt the anger that I had with Paulie and that helped motivate him as well. He didn't know if he had been sold down the river also, and he wasn't taking any chances.

His fight, a quick one also, lasted until midway through round three, and Smith never really got untracked. This time Billy dominated Delroy from the opening bell and it was only a matter of time before he found his opening to land the overhand right, his Sunday punch.

Again, the Petrovic Brothers had their hands raised in victory at center ring on the same night.

I took a most-needed, quick shower while the press in our dressing room was interviewing Billy, and when I threw a towel around my waist and sat down to answer their questions as well. Paulie sat between us but remained unusually silent, obviously angry and deep in thought.

Billy had a slight cut on the bridge of his nose, but I was unmarked. Heck, I doubt that I was ever hit. The entire minute plus of the fight was nothing more than a blur.

"Who's next for you champ?" One reporter asked looking at me, as Billy grabbed a clean towel and headed for the shower.

"I'd like to fight Larry Jones. He's the top contender and I think that it would be a great match." Jones wasn't a big puncher, but he was a southpaw, and had the style that could make anyone look bad, and he had given Schultz his first loss early in his career.

I could see that response really ticked off Paulie, because he interrupted me by saying. "Get dis straight! I'm Tony's manager, and those type a questions should be addressed only ta me. I made him a world champion and I make all the decisions on Tony's career."

I was more than ready to announce to the assembled press that Paulie was now my ex-manager, but I was too happy to ruin the evening any further for Paulie, who had brought me and Billy to the title. I had to show him some loyalty; besides, I figured that when everyone cleared out of the dressing room, except Billy of course, I'd confront Paulie with it. At the very least, he deserved a chance to explain why he wanted me to lose. I figured that it had to be the mob, but even if it was, Paulie had to realize that I wasn't going to risk getting hurt just to keep his 'friends' happy.

On the other hand, maybe, just maybe, he had no other choice. I figured he should have a chance to explain. He deserved that much, before we fired his cheating ass.

The mob proved to be the reason that Paulie wanted me to lose, but for a slightly different reason. And after the press had cleared out, I sat Paulie and Billy down.

"Okay, Paulie. You know we're on to you. It's time to tell the truth! What the fuck is going on? We all know that you wanted me to lose tonight."

Paulie's face grew red, and he began to sweat again. "What da hell do ya mean, Tony? Ain't I your manager and trainer? What the hell makes ya think dat I would want ya to lose? I didn't bring you this far to lose. Why should I?

"Suppose you tell us, and if we don't get the whole truth, we're going to go out and find another manager/trainer and I guarantee your career will be shot all to hell. Hell, I just might even tell the press that you didn't bother to train me properly. You'll be all washed up in this business. So you'd better fess up!"

Billy looked surprised, but just nodded his agreement as Paulie glanced up at him, then back down to the tile dressing room floor. I knew that Billy would support anything I'd say or do.

Paulie raised his bowed head. "Okay, kids. Ya want da truth. I fucked up! I play da ponies a lot and I owe a bookie a lot of money, and I made a big bet on Schultz winning ta try to get even."

There were tears welling up in Paulie's eyes as he looked at both of us and continued.

"I'm sorry, boys. I didn't mean to hurt ya. Ya have to know that much. But these guys play rough. They don't follow the same rules like we do in boxing. They use baseball bats and lead pipes instead of gloves, and they don't mind kicking or hitting below da belt as often as needed. I still don't know how I'm going to pay em back. I also bet on Billy and if he didn't win, it would be twice as much money I owe these guys. It was a one-shot deal, and I was gonna make ya a champ again, honest!"

"But why the hell didn't you bet on me to win? Didn't you think I could take him?" I asked.

"Well, I knew dat I had no control of Schultz, who is bigger and stronger than you, and I figured if you fought as badly as you did against him in your

177

first fight against him, or worse, he'd be an easy winner. I figured if I didn't train ya right, I'd be able to get out of da hole."

I glanced up at Billy, who knew me well enough to realize that I would never make this kind of a fuss unless I knew that I was right. He just looked at Paulie and silently shook his head, letting me make the big decisions and do the talking for both of us, as I usually did.

Paulie continued to look down at the concrete floor, unable to face us. "So kids, what are ya gonna do now, go to the press, find another manager, or what? Whatever ya do, I know dat I deserve it. I really fucked up dis time!"

Billy looked at me, as if I had some magic answer. He knew full well that loyalty was always a strong trait of mine.

"Tell you what, Paulie," I said, "I don't like what you did tonight and right now I don't even like you one bit. In fact I think that you're a real asshole!

Paulie, sweating profusely, bowed his head in shame.

"And Billy and I may never be able to forgive you for this, or completely trust you again. But you did take us in and teach us the skills we needed to become world champions. So we do owe you for that. Maybe Billy and I can give you an advance on our purses and bail you out, this time ONLY!

And you can pay us back by taking a smaller percentage of our fights, until the loan is all paid off. But no more gambling. If we find out that you fucked up just once, the press finds out and you're history with us."

Billy sat silently, while Paulie still had his head facing the floor. "After what I just tried to do to ya, ya guys would really do dis fer me?"

"Yes, on the condition that this is a one-time only happening. And if you ever try to get either of us to lose a fight again, no matter how much trouble you're in. You can find yourselves some other fighters to lose, because we don't intend to. You have a problem again, you come to us first. Agreed?"

"I owe the books more then three thousand bucks, Tony."

That was a lot of money back then. Billy and I did have a lot of other expenses.

I looked at Billy and he just nodded. "Okay, Paulie, we'll loan you whatever you need, but just this once. And instead of taking twenty percent of our purses, you take fifteen percent until the entire loan is repaid."

Paulie finally looked up at me. 'You guys would really do dat fer me?' He repeated. He seemed to be almost in tears again.

"Don't start crying. We did lose a lot of respect for you tonight, as a person, but you do know the boxing game. You're going to have to earn our trust again. But, we owe you also." I said. "Now how much money do you need?"

"Thirty seven hundred bucks and I need it tonight or I may not be around tomorrow."

"What about your cut of our purses?" Billy inquired. "Doesn't that cover it?"

"Dat money I owe them is after I get my percentage. I still need thirty seven hundred smackers more".

I did some quick math. "That's eighteen fifty each. Okay with you, Billy?"

Billy said. 'Okay, but just this once. Mary can never find out about it or she'll divorce me. And Paulie, if you ever try to get either Tony or me hurt again, you'll be wishing that those bookmakers had the first crack at you, because we're going to kick your ass from here to Kingdom Come and then back again.

Paulie looked directly into Billy's cold, steel blue eyes and knew he that he wasn't joking.

"I swear to ya guys, on my life, dis will never happen again."

"It will be your life if it does," Billy said as he finished dressing.

It never would happen again.

I called the hospital from the dressing room first, to find out that Schultz, while still alive, was on life support and in the intensive care unit. That news really took a lot out of my victory.

And the thought did cross my mind that if it wasn't for Paulie trying to get me to lose, Schultz' injury might never have happened. It certainly put a damper on another otherwise very successful evening. Of course I also knew that if I didn't catch on when I had, I might no longer be a world champion. The more I thought about it, the angrier I got at Paulie, but I gave my word and I would never go back on it.

And, I thought, it could have been me in the hospital, fighting for my life, instead of Schultz.

I told Billy that I had to go to the hospital to see Schultz, and that I'd meet him back at the house. His wife and daughter were at his bedside, but they refused to look at me or accept my apology.

The doctor at the hospital told me that even if Schultz lived, he'd be little more than a vegetable. His life or death would be in God's hands now. I said a silent prayer and left. It took a lot of soul searching and a few tears before I was ready to return home.

First Billy and I called home to tell our wives the great news, but the radio and our neighbors had already informed them, and they were very excited. But any real party would have to be put off for a few days, as the weather was very bad and we wanted to celebrate with family and friends. But Jodie and I did decide to try to make a baby that night to celebrate.

This time we earned $25,000 apiece and that was our largest purse to date.

That was the good news. The bad news was that four days after the fight, Schultz, who never regained consciousness, passed away with a massive cerebral hemorrhage. Talk about your post fight letdowns, and even though I had expected it, I was still devastated.

I knew in my heart that it wasn't my fault. I went out there and did what I intended to do, end it early. I could have blamed Paulie, but I knew that he was not responsible either. Sure, he bet on the fight, but he certainly didn't set it up for me to win. And no one could ever have expected the tragedy that occurred.

I could have also blamed it on the referee, but I figure he also knew that he screwed up and should have stopped the fight sooner. And that he had to live with the guilt as well. I don't think he was crooked, just incompetent.

But I was the one who threw the punches and now I had to live with the outcome for the rest of my life. Even today, I think about Schultz just lying in the hospital bed, tubes running into his mouth and nose, and God only knows where else. And I still wonder what became of his family. I wanted to send them some money to help out, but because I had to bail Paulie out, I didn't have enough left.

I guess this fight was the last time that Paulie called me 'Killer' which he had nicknamed me just before I had won the title. It was just in very poor taste at this point, and I didn't like it anymore than he did.

Mary, although happy for Billy was not a big fight fan. And her attitude got worse when she learned that Schultz had died. "What if it was you, Billy, you're human also. It could have been you in the ring that night? Isn't it time you gave some consideration to your family? We need you!"

Mary was always worrying that something bad was going to happen to him in the ring, and the death of Schultz only added to the worry. And while Mary always would sit on the edge of her seat listening to all his fights on the radio, she never wanted to be anywhere in or even near the arena when Billy fought. She wanted him to find a job in a different line of work, but knew that he'd never come close to bringing home the type of money that being a world champion brought, and with a growing family, Mary knew that the money that goes with the title, was going to be needed.

I suppose you could say in fairness, that Mary did make an effort, sort of… Shortly after their marriage, Billy talked Mary into going into the gym to watch them work out. She was there long enough to remark about how badly the place stank of sweat, before Paulie told her that 'boxing is a man's sport and no dames were ever allowed in the gym.'

Billy and I urged Paulie to let her stay, but you could easily see that Mary was upset by the whole thing and wanted to leave as quickly as possible. We understood and didn't try to stop her.

Mary wanted us to take our purse money and open a business together. Her thought was a small restaurant. Both Mary and Jodie were great cooks and no one would dare to bounce a check with Billy and me on hand. Besides, our names would also help draw a lot of customers from the boxing community.

It wasn't really a bad idea, and we did talk it over at length, but it was going to be on the condition that Billy would remain in the ring until we were sure the business was going to make it. And that didn't do anything to gladden Mary's heart very much. 'I don't understand boxing', she would say. 'Why can't these guys earn a legitimate living instead of trying to bash the brains out of their opponents? There are plenty of other ways to make a decent living, and after what happened to poor Bill Schultz…For Pete's sake Billy, you could get yourself killed just as easily. Where would that leave me and Billy Jr.?

"Do you remember Uncle Johnny," Billy always replied. "He worked in the coal mines and all he got as a result of all that hard work and sweat was black lung disease, which eventually killed him. He coughed constantly, and I know that it annoyed our Aunt Jen. Mary, you can get killed in any profession. You can get killed crossing the street. We couldn't earn this kind of money anywhere else so please don't blame boxing for improving our lifestyle."

Trying to reason with Mary was never an easy task, she was very stubborn, and after a long hesitation, she gave up on trying to change our minds, and the restaurant idea was put on the back burner for the time being.

And the fact that Mary was didn't seem to be completely in his corner depressed Billy. I know that they argued about it a lot, because Jodie had told me.

Jodie didn't like boxing that much either. Because of the fact that she was brought up with it, she tolerated it a lot more than Mary did. As she put it "My dad boxed and mom was always in his corner. I made a commitment to always be by your side, and I intend to keep it. Till death do us part. If it's the way you choose to make a living, Tony, so be it."

I suppose that over the years a little of Mary's negativity did wear off a bit on Jodie, but her support for me and what I did for a living never wavered. She always remembered what her mom went through when her dad was boxing for a living. I couldn't have found a better wife.

Not that Mary was a bad person for caring about Billy's health and life. If she didn't care she wouldn't have been human. Her emotions were very understandable, but I do believe that she should have been more like Jodie and supported her husband in and out of the ring. Although, I never voiced that view to Billy and thinking back, maybe, I should have.

We started taking fights on different cards so that Billy or I could remain at home to take care of our growing families, although more often than not, Jodie came with me and sat at ringside when I fought. Billy didn't have that kind of support group, although Jodie came to most of his fights, and I worked his corner to give him some support and save some money on hiring a cut man. There was really no danger, as Billy never had sustained a serious cut in any of his fights, and never would.

In September, Billy finally had his first loss, but it was in a non-title bout. It was just one of those fights that Billy didn't take seriously enough. He didn't train hard enough, and took his opponent for granted, which, when looking at his opponents won-loss record, was easy to do.

As a result he ran out of steam in the seventh round, and lost a decision at Madison Square Garden in NY, in a non-title match, to a George O'Conner, who was not highly thought of at the time, or any other time for that matter. It was Billy's first loss in 34 fights, and he had 30 knockouts during that time. Not Technical Knockouts by the way, but the real one-punch variety type. Fortunately he kept his title, but now a rematch with O'Conner, for the title, was scheduled for the Garden on November ninth.

This time Billy trained like a man possessed. He did more roadwork than he ever did before. I tried, but even I couldn't come close to keeping up with his frenzied pace. He wanted revenge for his only defeat and had no intention of losing his title.

I only had four fights in 1946, taking some time off to be with Jodie and enjoy my new lifestyle. I won them all, and although I could have fought on the undercard of Billy's return match with O'Conner, I passed it up. We didn't really need the money at that point, and I was looking forward to a match with an Olympic Gold Medalist, Wendell Jordan, who had won sixteen out of sixteen fights since turning pro. While he wasn't quite ready to fight fifteen rounders yet, he was a crowd favorite. Jordan kept calling me out, and I knew that sooner or later we'd have to fight.

But that fight wasn't going to happen for another year.

I worked the corner as a cut man, for Billy's return match with George O'Conner. Billy was anxious to get revenge, and it almost cost him the title.

Paulie gave him instructions before the fight. He told Billy to 'work the body till his hands came down, then look for an opportunity to throw that big right.'

Billy had his own personal vendetta and was anxious to show to the world that his first fight with O'Conner was a fluke. As a 7-1 favorite, Billy really didn't have a lot to prove to the fans.

Instead of following Paulies instructions and working over O'Conners body, Billy started head hunting from the opening bell, and no matter how much Paulie would plead with him, that he was tiring himself out by throwing haymakers that were often off target or punches that O'Conner was easily picking off with his gloves.

It wasn't till the fourth round that Paulie had to slap Billy in the face to get his attention. "C'mon Billy, ya want to lose the fucking title? This fight is for your belt! The belt you've worked so long and hard fer. Do you want to lose it to a stiff like this? Whatsa matta with ya? Where's your pride? Now listen to me, work da body! You'll get ya chance for the knockout when his guard comes down, and it will. Ya making a very easy fight look hard."

"Listen to him, Billy," I chimed in. "Paulies right. Look at that big stomach of his. It's an easy target. You couldn't miss it if you tried. Work the body, he'll cave in. He's way out of shape. You're making this guy look like a world champion."

Billy finally listened, and two rounds later O'Conner started dropping his hands, giving Billy the opportunity he needed to land a big overhand right to the temple. It shouldn't have taken Billy six rounds for the knockout, and I knew Paulie would be all over him for not listening early on. I also knew that Billy had earned the lecture that surely was coming.

But first it was time to celebrate, and we all went out for a few beers. But the party ended quickly when Billy called home and found that his wife, Mary, had taken Billy Jr. to the hospital, with a very high fever.

We called a cab, and had the driver take us to the hospital, where Mary and Jodie awaited.

Billy Jr. had pneumonia and was coughing. The emergency doctor assured us that this wasn't a life or death situation, but they did keep him overnight for observation, and we all remained until the sun was starting to come up, when the hospital finally finished treating my nephew and released him. It was daylight by the time we finally reached out home.

Chapter VI

1946, marked the first session of the newly formed United Nations in New York City. It also brought into the open the horrific acts of Nazi Germany in the concentration camps, with the Nuremberg Trials, and the hanging of most of the leaders of the mass exterminations of Jews and Gypsies, probably including much of our family. The vivid images of the death camps still linger in my mind.

And in boxing, former world heavyweight champion Jack Johnson was killed in a car accident in North Carolina.

But for Billy and I, it was to be business as usual. After the wedding and reception, Billy and I immediately went back into serious training for our next title defenses. It didn't seem right not being able to have a honeymoon, but everyone knew that it would come in the future, when time and money was not to be a factor.

We were training for what was to be an exact rematch, bout wise, of our first title fight card, since almost everybody thought that Delroy Smith would have beaten Billy if he had just been able to stay away from his power.

Maybe Smith could have won the decision, but staying away from a fast, big puncher like my brother, for fifteen rounds, was never an easy task, even for a slick, jab and move fighter like Delroy Smith.

I didn't realize it till many years later, because Billy had never told anyone, (it was one of the few things he kept from me) but he had begun getting many life threatening letters and calls for fighting against a black fighter, who never had the same opportunity in any sport that the white man did, back then. But boxing was the one sport that was in the forefront of racial equality in sports, and rightly so.

Racism was still part of America's legacy, and many white Southerners were continuing to fight the Civil War, and hoping that 'the South would indeed rise again.' The Klu Klux Clan was still going strong, preaching their hatred. Although I don't recall any of the neo-Nazi skinheads being around back then. I guess hate has been and always will be part of our world, although I believe it's more a statement of jealousy of those who have not, against those who have.

The only reason I was able to find out about the threats, was through all of the hate mail and notes that Billy had kept well hidden, so Mary wouldn't find out and cause him further grief in furthering his boxing career.

It was strange, that I fought Bob Harrison a couple of times but never received any threats. But the truth is, I never had any threats.. The reason

192

may have been that these fights were held in "The City of Brotherly Love", and not South of the Mason Dixon Line.

Neither Billy nor I ever learned or understood prejudice at our home or in school. We knew that it was going on in the South, and that blacks were treated as second class citizens, via Jim Crow laws, but we never fully realized the full extent of it, until Billy decided to take a fight in Charleston, South Carolina.

I know that if Mary would have found out about the letters, Billy probably would have been forced to stop boxing and change professions, and he might still be alive today. Hindsight is always 20-20. Billy, like myself, never had any use for prejudice. To us it was plain stupidity. It didn't belong in life or in any sport, and certainly not in boxing, where everyone was equal when the bell rings.

Mom and Uncle Johnny had brought us up to respect everyone, and that's exactly what we did. Hate was a four-letter word that should only have been found in the dictionary, if that, and not in our everyday vocabulary. Besides, how could you not respect anyone who had the courage to step into the ring with you and slug it out, one on one? That courage alone deserves an enormous amount of respect. And every boxer we had fought we respected and I assume vice-versa.

Sure, we would always read about how bad the blacks were being treated down South, having to use separate toilets, water fountains, and eat in segregated restaurants. We knew that as stupid as it was, the fact that blacks had to ride in the back of busses existed in the south. But reading about it and seeing it first hand were two different things.

We also realized that blacks weren't able to get the type of quality education that a white man could. There seemed to be very little that we could do to improve their lot in life, which would finally start to improve during the Kennedy administration. The use of 'affirmative action' was also helpful, although I'm not sure we still need that today. We did, make open statements to the press that we completely supported all those brave folks who were fighting for the rights of the black folks in the South. We had even discussed the possibility of becoming 'freedom marchers' and help lead the fight for equality.

It was a very sad time in our history. These mistreated minorities in the Southern States didn't really ask for much, mainly equality. They wanted to be treated exactly like any other human being. And why not? They are no different than anyone else.

I remember once stopping by a restaurant in Southern Maryland when I was younger. I can't remember much of the details, but I can vividly recall a sign on the door of the establishment, it read 'No colored or dogs allowed'. This was the lot of many blacks living in the South in the mid 20th century, and slavery had already been dead more than 100 years, at least legally. Talk about man's inhumanity to man.

I was going to fight Bill Schultz again. I figured I owed him the rematch due to the head-butt, which I knew that I had caused, although it was not intentional on my part. A fight should be won or lost legally. And I had fouled Schultz, that much I knew.

Fortunately, the real fight fans also raised a bit of an uproar in favor of the rematch, so despite Paulie's initial objections that Schultz was still much too strong for me, the money was right and he allowed the fight to go on.

I thought it was a bit odd that Paulie was not having me do much roadwork or shadow boxing for the rematch, even though he at first told me that Schultz was too big and strong for me.

And he never showed me how to turn Bill Schultz around, as he had promised to, after our first fight. When I asked him about it, he just said "Ya don't have to knock yourself out, Tony, I was wrong. I really think that it's gonna be a very easy fight for ya. Ya really learned a lot in your first fight with Schultz." Strange, I thought, Paulie always had me working hard no matter how easy the opponent was supposed to be. At first he didn't even want me to take this fight. I figured that maybe the word was out that Schultz was going into the tank, and I didn't have to do much to win. I wanted to be wrong, and I was. Boy was I wrong.

But for now who was I to argue? Paulie was the boss and had been around the boxing business long before I was born. He knew which end was up and he had always made sure Billy and I had been well taken care of.

This double championship fight card took place on February 11, 1946, and once again at the Philadelphia Coliseum. I didn't think it was possible to get more attendance at this fight, as there was a major snowstorm blowing and powerful, freezing gusts of wind which would surely would prevent even the most diehard fight fans from coming out.

But fight fans again proved to be a hearty breed, and if there was an empty seat in the house, neither Billy nor I could see it.

After a few quick prelims, there was a loud knock on the dressing room door. "Tony, you're up next."

This was very odd. I thought I was supposed to be fighting the main event, I always had before. Then I thought that maybe Billy's fight must have fallen out. I looked at Paulie for some insight. He had a surprised look on his face but could only shrug his shoulders. "Ya know as much as I do. They musta figured they'll save the bigger puncher for the main event. You know how excited fans get about seein' the knockout. I guess they decided to put ya on first, Tony".

I didn't even have my hands wrapped yet, and I hadn't come close to have broken a sweat. Even the trainers of today will always tell you that you never should go into a fight 'cold' or 'dry'.

As Paulie was quickly wrapping my hands Billy told the security guard at the door that we needed about five more minutes. The realization then suddenly occurred to me, Paulie didn't really want me to win this fight. He had either made a bet on my opponent or was back in with the mob, maybe both. That would certainly explain why I went from a 2-1 betting favorite to a 5-2 underdog on fight day. That was the information (the odds) that was reported in the local paper that morning.

I suddenly had this urge to shove Paulie's unlit cigar down his grizzled throat. But instead I figured out that we still needed him, and besides, Billy was up next. I kept my rage inside, knowing that poor Bill Schultz, like our last fight, was going to get the worst of it. I took a deep breath to try to relax. I knew that I didn't even have to work up a sweat to have the hatred and energy to destroy Schultz and teach Paulie a lesson he'd never forget. Nothing was going to stop me! Nothing!

Paulie quickly finished wrapping my hands with adhesive tape, and lacing up the gloves, adding the white tape to keep them secure to my wrists. Billy walked over and patted my butt to wish me luck, and I called him aside and whispered to him what my suspicions were. Then I said, "luck? I don't need luck! Schultz does. If I'm right, I need a quick knockout and Billy, I'm going to get one tonight!"

"No fuckin way! I don't believe it!" Billy shouted, loud enough for everyone in the dressing room, including Paulie to hear. Hell, it was probably loud enough for Schultz in the next dressing room to overhear. He glared at Paulie, shook his head, but said nothing to him.

"You have to trust me on this one, Billy" I said quietly. I'll explain after the fight. And believe me, I am going to make it a quick one. The way Paulie trained me, or rather didn't for this fight, I'm going to have to."

Paulie sensed that there was something different about the way I walked and spoke, (in truth I deliberately swaggered with confidence, which is something that I had never done before) down the aisle, a snarl instead of a smile upon my face. And I wasn't waving back to the fans, as I had become accustomed to doing in my previous fights.

I wasn't interested in anything more than taking all my frustrations out on my opponent, and I intended to give it my all from the first bell. I realized that I hadn't trained for 15 rounds and the only way I was going to win this fight was by a quick knockout. This was either going to be a very fast win for me, and Paulie was going to learn a lesson tonight, or I was going to get the ass kicking of my life, I thought.

"Are ya okay, Tony? Ya acting kinda funny," Paulie asked, over the roar of the large crowd. He probably noticed that my demeanor was a lot different than usual. I was hoping that he would see that.

"Never felt better in my entire life, Paulie. I'm ready for this fight, and I'm going to really kick some serious butt tonight. I'm going to take this guy out early. He'll never know what hit him. You really motivated me well, Paulie. I'm definitely up for this fight." I replied. Knowing that those words would probably upset him far more than anything else I could do or say at that moment.

And it must have done exactly that, because Paulie started to look at me strangely. He had never before seen me this confidant, I felt that he had to know or at least suspect that I was on to him. He reached up with his free hand and mopped his sweaty brow with his shirtsleeve. "Don't go for the early KO, Tony. That's a mistake. He's too strong. Just wear him down like I trained ya to".

I shook my head. "No Paulie, I feel way too good tonight. This fight is going to be very short and sweet".

Paulie responded with something. But I covered my ears indicating that because of the crowd noise I could not hear him. I knew that he was trying to talk me into fighting the fight his way, which could mean me losing and maybe even getting hurt, and that was not going to happen.

199

So despite the coolness of the arena, Paulie actually began to sweat all over, staining the armpit area of his shirt. It wasn't hot or humid in the arena, so I figured that my ideas about Paulie intending to double cross us had proved correct. I knew full well that he was no longer in my corner, and maybe was not going to be in Billy's either. And I knew that taking any advice from him at this point would be like asking him the easiest way on how to lose the fight and my title.

We reached the ring and I quickly ducked under the top strand of rope to get inside. I stepped into the box of resin that was always in the corners in those days to prevent a fighter from slipping. They don't use resin boxes today.

I had made up my mind as we walked down the aisle that this fight was going to be over in the first round. I decided that well before Paulie said 'Easy fight, Tony. Ya ready for him. Now, just take ya time and wear him down gradually. He got nuthin and ain't nothin' to worry about.'

I found it hard to believe that he was actually telling me all this bullshit with a straight face. He really sounded sincere. Still there was little doubt in my mind that Paulie had sold me out and maybe my kid brother as well. Even if I was wrong about Paulie, I knew that because of my insufficient training, I needed the early knockout.

We received the referee's instructions at center ring, staring each other down. We touched gloves and I went back to my corner, jumping up and down to try to work up a sweat. I really didn't want to waste any of my pent-up energy and I knew I was never that big a puncher. But I knew today that I had better have learned how to turn over a punch.

Schultz and I were both wearing what looked to be the same trunks that we wore in our first fight, minus the blood and sweat, of course.

The bell rang and we touched gloves again. As soon as we met in center ring I tore into Schultz like I never tore into anyone before, or since, in or out of the ring. I was throwing every punch I could, in every direction and angle possible, with his head being the main target.

I realize that there was some danger in giving Schultz an opening, but I figured there would be far more risk if I gave him the chance to recover and drag the fight on. I knew I hadn't trained for a long fight. Besides, I was never known as being a fast starter, and I hoped this tactic would surprise him. It did, and Paulie too.

Quickly I had muscled him back against the ropes, pounding away, and he had no way to escape the onslaught. I continued throwing punches from every angle. His legs suddenly seemed to be made of jelly, but why wasn't he going down? Maybe the ropes were holding him up. Why wasn't the referee jumping in between us and stopping the fight? Was he blind or did he also bet on Schultz?

I wanted this win badly, but I certainly didn't intend to kill my opponent. I kept thinking that the ref had to be in on the fix too? I yelled at the ref to stop the fight, but he just stood back and ignored me. If he was bought and paid for also, I was determined that like Paulie, he wasn't going to collect this bet.

I didn't take a lot of time to think about it. I turned over a solid overhand right, which landed flush on Schultz' temple and he went down like a rock hitting water. I think it was the hardest punch I had ever thrown and I knew immediately that he wasn't going to beat the count, and judging by the loud roar, the crowd knew it as well. It was all over at 1:16 of the first round.

In truth, with all the anger I had inside me at the time, I think the fight was over well before the first bell had rung.

I found out later that I had thrown more punches in 76 seconds than in any entire 3-minute round in my ring career.

The fight had ended, and the crowd was roaring so loud, I could hardly hear myself think. Then I noticed, while the referee was raising my hand in victory, Schultz was still lying flat on his back, his corner team and the fight doctor surrounding him. A stretcher and oxygen tank was called for and Schultz was taken to a nearby hospital by ambulance.

Billy was supposed to be the big puncher in the family, how on earth did this happen? I thought to myself. Where did all that power suddenly come from? It had to be the adrenaline. In truth Paulie helped me win this fight, more then he would ever know.

I turned to Paulie who seemed to be as red-faced as I had ever seen him, and immediately knew that my suspicions about him were correct.

I had wanted to knock Schultz out, but I had no intention of hurting him badly. I began to worry. 'What if I had killed him?' No win in the world would ever be worth having to live with that on my conscience for the rest of my life. Why was that damn piece of shit referee so slow in jumping in?

Not knowing if Schultz was going to make it or not took some of the edge off the win, I had wanted so badly.

And it came as no surprise that Paulie's negative attitude wasn't exactly what you'd call 'congratulatory'. "Nice work, Tony. But what da fuck were you doin' out there? I'm your trainer. Ya supposed to follow my instructions. I told you to take your time and wear him down. Look what you did to him. You mighta killed him. Whatsa matta, with ya, can't ya hear? What the fuck am I training ya for? Don't ya ever fuckin listen? They're taking Schultz out on a stretcher. I'm really disappointed in ya."

Paulie always talked fast and his East Coast slang could easily be picked up, especially when he was angry.

I was just about to tell Paulie that he was through talking and was fired, and to take a long walk on a short pier, but I has to hold back. I just couldn't do that with Billy's fight up next. I really think that if he wasn't so old I could have sent him into the balcony with one punch. But I couldn't leave my little brother without a manager or a corner.

And I wasn't going to make any move until I spoke to Billy. We always decided things together. I was just hoping that Paulie wasn't trying to get Billy to lose also, but figured that he wasn't because Billy had trained properly for his fight.

I admit the thought did cross my mind that if Paulie had lost some money on me, he could try to recoup his losses by betting against Billy. Then I figured that unless he had done so prior to the fight, he wouldn't have the time to do so now and he had trained Billy correctly.

The sound of a bell ringing brought me quickly back to reality.

"His corner should have thrown in the towel, or the ref should have had brains enough to stop the damn fight", I replied. "We all saw that I was kicking his ass, big time! It was a no-contest. Thanks Paulie, you really trained me well for this one."

I knew the words had stung him.

Billy was walking slowly down the aisle towards the ring, waving to the crowd, and I was walking the other way, towards the dressing room, also acknowledging the cheers.

When we passed each other, he had a big smile on his face. "Great fight, Tony", he said as we touched hands.

"Go get 'em, Billy, take him out early. We have a lot of celebrating to do", I yelled loud enough for Paulie to hear. Paulie turned and gave me a dirty look, but quickly and quietly left my side and walked back towards the ring with Billy.

I waited by the radio, anxiously waiting to listen to Billy's fight, before taking my shower. I had worked up a heavy sweat in a very short time, and really needed the shower, but I needed to hear all of Billy's fight.

Hopefully Paulie would have the decency to have him ready to win. And I also was awaiting news about Bill Schultz, who was now in the hospital. Besides, Delroy Smith was not known as a very big puncher.

And Billy had learned a lot from his first fight with Smith, and now with a child at home, he had that extra fire in the belly, the incentive that you often need to keep you going, the extra edge given by motivation.

Of course he too felt the anger that I had with Paulie and that helped motivate him as well. He didn't know if he had been sold down the river also, and he wasn't taking any chances.

His fight, a quick one also, lasted until midway through round three, and Smith never really got untracked. This time Billy dominated Delroy from the opening bell and it was only a matter of time before he found his opening to land the overhand right, his Sunday punch.

Again, the Petrovic Brothers had their hands raised in victory at center ring on the same night.

I took a most-needed, quick shower while the press in our dressing room was interviewing Billy, and when I threw a towel around my waist and sat down to answer their questions as well. Paulie sat between us but remained unusually silent, obviously angry and deep in thought.

Billy had a slight cut on the bridge of his nose, but I was unmarked. Heck, I doubt that I was ever hit. The entire minute plus of the fight was nothing more than a blur.

"Who's next for you champ?" One reporter asked looking at me, as Billy grabbed a clean towel and headed for the shower.

"I'd like to fight Larry Jones. He's the top contender and I think that it would be a great match." Jones wasn't a big puncher, but he was a southpaw, and had the style that could make anyone look bad, and he had given Schultz his first loss early in his career.

I could see that response really ticked off Paulie, because he interrupted me by saying. "Get dis straight! I'm Tony's manager, and those type a questions should be addressed only ta me. I made him a world champion and I make all the decisions on Tony's career."

I was more than ready to announce to the assembled press that Paulie was now my ex-manager, but I was too happy to ruin the evening any further for Paulie, who had brought me and Billy to the title. I had to show him some loyalty; besides, I figured that when everyone cleared out of the dressing room, except Billy of course, I'd confront Paulie with it. At the very least, he deserved a chance to explain why he wanted me to lose. I figured that it had to be the mob, but even if it was, Paulie had to realize that I wasn't going to risk getting hurt just to keep his 'friends' happy.

207

On the other hand, maybe, just maybe, he had no other choice. I figured he should have a chance to explain. He deserved that much, before we fired his cheating ass.

The mob proved to be the reason that Paulie wanted me to lose, but for a slightly different reason. And after the press had cleared out, I sat Paulie and Billy down.

"Okay, Paulie. You know we're on to you. It's time to tell the truth! What the fuck is going on? We all know that you wanted me to lose tonight."

Paulie's face grew red, and he began to sweat again. "What da hell do ya mean, Tony? Ain't I your manager and trainer? What the hell makes ya think dat I would want ya to lose? I didn't bring you this far to lose. Why should I?

"Suppose you tell us, and if we don't get the whole truth, we're going to go out and find another manager/trainer and I guarantee your career will be shot all to hell. Hell, I just might even tell the press that you didn't bother to train me properly. You'll be all washed up in this business. So you'd better fess up!"

Billy looked surprised, but just nodded his agreement as Paulie glanced up at him, then back down to the tile dressing room floor. I knew that Billy would support anything I'd say or do.

Paulie raised his bowed head. "Okay, kids. Ya want da truth. I fucked up! I play da ponies a lot and I owe a bookie a lot of money, and I made a big bet on Schultz winning ta try to get even."

There were tears welling up in Paulie's eyes as he looked at both of us and continued.

"I'm sorry, boys. I didn't mean to hurt ya. Ya have to know that much. But these guys play rough. They don't follow the same rules like we do in boxing. They use baseball bats and lead pipes instead of gloves, and they don't mind kicking or hitting below da belt as often as needed. I still don't know how I'm going to pay em back. I also bet on Billy and if he didn't win, it would be twice as much money I owe these guys. It was a one-shot deal, and I was gonna make ya a champ again, honest!"

"But why the hell didn't you bet on me to win? Didn't you think I could take him?" I asked.

"Well, I knew dat I had no control of Schultz, who is bigger and stronger than you, and I figured if you fought as badly as you did against him in your first fight against him, or worse, he'd be an easy winner. I figured if I didn't train ya right, I'd be able to get out of da hole."

I glanced up at Billy, who knew me well enough to realize that I would never make this kind of a fuss unless I knew that I was right. He just looked at Paulie and silently shook his head, letting me make the big decisions and do the talking for both of us, as I usually did.

Paulie continued to look down at the concrete floor, unable to face us. "So kids, what are ya gonna do now, go to the press, find another manager, or what? Whatever ya do, I know dat I deserve it. I really fucked up dis time!"

Billy looked at me, as if I had some magic answer. He knew full well that loyalty was always a strong trait of mine.

"Tell you what, Paulie," I said, "I don't like what you did tonight and right now I don't even like you one bit. In fact I think that you're a real asshole!

Paulie, sweating profusely, bowed his head in shame.

"And Billy and I may never be able to forgive you for this, or completely trust you again. But you did take us in and teach us the skills we needed to become world champions. So we do owe you for that. Maybe Billy and I can give you an advance on our purses and bail you out, this time ONLY!

And you can pay us back by taking a smaller percentage of our fights, until the loan is all paid off. But no more gambling. If we find out that you fucked up just once, the press finds out and you're history with us."

Billy sat silently, while Paulie still had his head facing the floor. "After what I just tried to do to ya, ya guys would really do dis fer me?"

"Yes, on the condition that this is a one-time only happening. And if you ever try to get either of us to lose a fight again, no matter how much trouble you're in. You can find yourselves some other fighters to lose, because we don't intend to. You have a problem again, you come to us first. Agreed?"

"I owe the books more then three thousand bucks, Tony."

That was a lot of money back then. Billy and I did have a lot of other expenses.

I looked at Billy and he just nodded. "Okay, Paulie, we'll loan you whatever you need, but just this once. And instead of taking twenty percent of our purses, you take fifteen percent until the entire loan is repaid."

Paulie finally looked up at me. 'You guys would really do dat fer me?' He repeated. He seemed to be almost in tears again.

"Don't start crying. We did lose a lot of respect for you tonight, as a person, but you do know the boxing game. You're going to have to earn our trust again. But, we owe you also." I said. "Now how much money do you need?"

"Thirty seven hundred bucks and I need it tonight or I may not be around tomorrow."

"What about your cut of our purses?" Billy inquired. "Doesn't that cover it?"

"Dat money I owe them is after I get my percentage. I still need thirty seven hundred smackers more".

I did some quick math. "That's eighteen fifty each. Okay with you, Billy?"

Billy said. 'Okay, but just this once. Mary can never find out about it or she'll divorce me. And Paulie, if you ever try to get either Tony or me hurt again, you'll be wishing that those bookmakers had the first crack at you, because we're going to kick your ass from here to Kingdom Come and then back again.

Paulie looked directly into Billy's cold, steel blue eyes and knew he that he wasn't joking.

"I swear to ya guys, on my life, dis will never happen again."

"It will be your life if it does," Billy said as he finished dressing.

It never would happen again.

I called the hospital from the dressing room first, to find out that Schultz, while still alive, was on life support and in the intensive care unit. That news really took a lot out of my victory.

And the thought did cross my mind that if it wasn't for Paulie trying to get me to lose, Schultz' injury might never have happened. It certainly put a damper on another otherwise very successful evening. Of course I also knew that if I didn't catch on when I had, I might no longer be a world champion. The more I thought about it, the angrier I got at Paulie, but I gave my word and I would never go back on it.

And, I thought, it could have been me in the hospital, fighting for my life, instead of Schultz.

I told Billy that I had to go to the hospital to see Schultz, and that I'd meet him back at the house. His wife and daughter were at his bedside, but they refused to look at me or accept my apology.

213

The doctor at the hospital told me that even if Schultz lived, he'd be little more than a vegetable. His life or death would be in God's hands now. I said a silent prayer and left. It took a lot of soul searching and a few tears before I was ready to return home.

First Billy and I called home to tell our wives the great news, but the radio and our neighbors had already informed them, and they were very excited. But any real party would have to be put off for a few days, as the weather was very bad and we wanted to celebrate with family and friends. But Jodie and I did decide to try to make a baby that night to celebrate.

This time we earned $25,000 apiece and that was our largest purse to date.

That was the good news. The bad news was that four days after the fight, Schultz, who never regained consciousness, passed away with a massive cerebral hemorrhage. Talk about your post fight letdowns, and even though I had expected it, I was still devastated.

I knew in my heart that it wasn't my fault. I went out there and did what I intended to do, end it early. I could have blamed Paulie, but I knew that he was not responsible either. Sure, he bet on the fight, but he certainly didn't set it up for me to win. And no one could ever have expected the tragedy that occurred.

I could have also blamed it on the referee, but I figure he also knew that he screwed up and should have stopped the fight sooner. And that he had to live with the guilt as well. I don't think he was crooked, just incompetent.

But I was the one who threw the punches and now I had to live with the outcome for the rest of my life. Even today, I think about Schultz just lying in the hospital bed, tubes running into his mouth and nose, and God only knows where else. And I still wonder what became of his family. I wanted to send them some money to help out, but because I had to bail Paulie out, I didn't have enough left.

I guess this fight was the last time that Paulie called me 'Killer' which he had nicknamed me just before I had won the title. It was just in very poor taste at this point, and I didn't like it anymore than he did.

Mary, although happy for Billy was not a big fight fan. And her attitude got worse when she learned that Schultz had died. "What if it was you, Billy, you're human also. It could have been you in the ring that night? Isn't it time you gave some consideration to your family? We need you!"

Mary was always worrying that something bad was going to happen to him in the ring, and the death of Schultz only added to the worry. And while Mary always would sit on the edge of her seat listening to all his fights on the radio, she never wanted to be anywhere in or even near the arena when Billy fought. She wanted him to find a job in a different line of work, but

215

knew that he'd never come close to bringing home the type of money that being a world champion brought, and with a growing family, Mary knew that the money that goes with the title, was going to be needed.

I suppose you could say in fairness, that Mary did make an effort, sort of… Shortly after their marriage, Billy talked Mary into going into the gym to watch them work out. She was there long enough to remark about how badly the place stank of sweat, before Paulie told her that 'boxing is a man's sport and no dames were ever allowed in the gym.'

Billy and I urged Paulie to let her stay, but you could easily see that Mary was upset by the whole thing and wanted to leave as quickly as possible. We understood and didn't try to stop her.

Mary wanted us to take our purse money and open a business together. Her thought was a small restaurant. Both Mary and Jodie were great cooks and no one would dare to bounce a check with Billy and me on hand. Besides, our names would also help draw a lot of customers from the boxing community.

It wasn't really a bad idea, and we did talk it over at length, but it was going to be on the condition that Billy would remain in the ring until we were sure the business was going to make it. And that didn't do anything to gladden Mary's heart very much. 'I don't understand boxing', she would say. 'Why can't these guys earn a legitimate living instead of trying to bash the brains out of their opponents? There are plenty of other ways to make a decent living, and after what happened to poor Bill Schultz…For Pete's sake Billy, you could get yourself killed just as easily. Where would that leave me and Billy Jr.?

"Do you remember Uncle Johnny," Billy always replied. "He worked in the coal mines and all he got as a result of all that hard work and sweat was black lung disease, which eventually killed him. He coughed constantly, and I know that it annoyed our Aunt Jen. Mary, you can get killed in any profession. You can get killed crossing the street. We couldn't earn this kind of money anywhere else so please don't blame boxing for improving our lifestyle."

Trying to reason with Mary was never an easy task, she was very stubborn, and after a long hesitation, she gave up on trying to change our minds, and the restaurant idea was put on the back burner for the time being.

And the fact that Mary was didn't seem to be completely in his corner depressed Billy. I know that they argued about it a lot, because Jodie had told me.

Jodie didn't like boxing that much either. Because of the fact that she was brought up with it, she tolerated it a lot more than Mary did. As she put it "My dad boxed and mom was always in his corner. I made a commitment to always be by your side, and I intend to keep it. Till death do us part. If it's the way you choose to make a living, Tony, so be it."

I suppose that over the years a little of Mary's negativity did wear off a bit on Jodie, but her support for me and what I did for a living never wavered. She always remembered what her mom went through when her dad was boxing for a living. I couldn't have found a better wife.

Not that Mary was a bad person for caring about Billy's health and life. If she didn't care she wouldn't have been human. Her emotions were very understandable, but I do believe that she should have been more like Jodie and supported her husband in and out of the ring. Although, I never voiced that view to Billy and thinking back, maybe, I should have.

We started taking fights on different cards so that Billy or I could remain at home to take care of our growing families, although more often than not, Jodie came with me and sat at ringside when I fought. Billy didn't have that kind of support group, although Jodie came to most of his fights, and I worked his corner to give him some support and save some money on hiring a cut man. There was really no danger, as Billy never had sustained a serious cut in any of his fights, and never would.

In September, Billy finally had his first loss, but it was in a non-title bout. It was just one of those fights that Billy didn't take seriously enough. He didn't train hard enough, and took his opponent for granted, which, when looking at his opponents won-loss record, was easy to do.

As a result he ran out of steam in the seventh round, and lost a decision at Madison Square Garden in NY, in a non-title match, to a George O'Conner, who was not highly thought of at the time, or any other time for that matter. It was Billy's first loss in 34 fights, and he had 30 knockouts during that time. Not Technical Knockouts by the way, but the real one-punch variety type. Fortunately he kept his title, but now a rematch with O'Conner, for the title, was scheduled for the Garden on November ninth.

This time Billy trained like a man possessed. He did more roadwork than he ever did before. I tried, but even I couldn't come close to keeping up with his frenzied pace. He wanted revenge for his only defeat and had no intention of losing his title.

I only had four fights in 1946, taking some time off to be with Jodie and enjoy my new lifestyle. I won them all, and although I could have fought on the undercard of Billy's return match with O'Conner, I passed it up. We didn't really need the money at that point, and I was looking forward to a match with an Olympic Gold Medalist, Wendell Jordan, who had won sixteen out of sixteen fights since turning pro. While he wasn't quite ready to fight fifteen rounders yet, he was a crowd favorite. Jordan kept calling me out, and I knew that sooner or later we'd have to fight.

Rusty Rubin

But that fight wasn't going to happen for another year.

I worked the corner as a cut man, for Billy's return match with George O'Conner. Billy was anxious to get revenge, and it almost cost him the title.

Paulie gave him instructions before the fight. He told Billy to 'work the body till his hands came down, then look for an opportunity to throw that big right.'

Billy had his own personal vendetta and was anxious to show to the world that his first fight with O'Conner was a fluke. As a 7-1 favorite, Billy really didn't have a lot to prove to the fans.

Instead of following Paulies instructions and working over O'Conners body, Billy started head hunting from the opening bell, and no matter how much Paulie would plead with him, that he was tiring himself out by throwing haymakers that were often off target or punches that O'Conner was easily picking off with his gloves.

It wasn't till the fourth round that Paulie had to slap Billy in the face to get his attention. "C'mon Billy, ya want to lose the fucking title? This fight is for your belt! The belt you've worked so long and hard fer. Do you want to lose it to a stiff like this? Whatsa matta with ya? Where's your pride? Now

220

listen to me, work da body! You'll get ya chance for the knockout when his guard comes down, and it will. Ya making a very easy fight look hard."

"Listen to him, Billy," I chimed in. "Paulies right. Look at that big stomach of his. It's an easy target. You couldn't miss it if you tried. Work the body, he'll cave in. He's way out of shape. You're making this guy look like a world champion."

Billy finally listened, and two rounds later O'Conner started dropping his hands, giving Billy the opportunity he needed to land a big overhand right to the temple. It shouldn't have taken Billy six rounds for the knockout, and I knew Paulie would be all over him for not listening early on. I also knew that Billy had earned the lecture that surely was coming.

But first it was time to celebrate, and we all went out for a few beers. But the party ended quickly when Billy called home and found that his wife, Mary, had taken Billy Jr. to the hospital, with a very high fever.

We called a cab, and had the driver take us to the hospital, where Mary and Jodie awaited.

Billy Jr. had pneumonia and was coughing. The emergency doctor assured us that this wasn't a life or death situation, but they did keep him overnight for observation, and we all remained until the sun was starting to come up,

Rusty Rubin

when the hospital finally finished treating my nephew and released him. It was daylight by the time we finally reached out home.

Chapter VII

1947 was a very tough year for Billy and the Petrolia family, but unquestionably far worse for Billy's wife and son. Billy Jr. took a longer time then expected to recover from the pneumonia, but thank God, he pulled through it just fine.

In the rest of the world, the peace treaty was signed in Paris, officially ending WWII. Jackie Robinson signed a contract to be the first black man to play baseball in the Major Leagues, with the Montreal Royals in the minors and the Brooklyn Dodgers in the 'bigs'. Billy Conn, one of my favorite fighters passed away.

A lot of guys were still getting discharged from the military and were coming back into the work force, and this included boxers who served their country with honor, many giving up prospective great careers to do so.

I was to fight ten times that year, winning all but one, which was called a draw, and although I though I had won that fight, protesting the decisions, unlike today, weren't at all common in those days. We let the reporters who saw the fight speak for us.

Of those nine wins, I only recorded two knockouts, however. Billy fought nine times, scoring nine knockouts, and all in five rounds or less. Billy was always a far bigger favorite with the fans than I would ever be. But there was no jealousy, just a lot of brotherly love and understanding. He was the puncher in the family, plain and simple. I was the boxer.

With the end of the war, a lot of ex-boxers returned to the ring, and the competition suddenly became a lot stiffer.

I'm not sure why I didn't have more KO's. Maybe it was the death of Billy Schultz that lay heavily on my conscience and made me tentative, or maybe because the adrenaline just wasn't flowing like it did in that one tragic fight. But it was probably more because I didn't have the power in my wrists and shoulders that Billy had.

I received a few stitches that year, but nothing really serious. It's just part of the price you sometimes have to pay to compete in your chosen profession. There's always a certain amount of extra risk in pro sports. No one ever told us that a career in boxing was going to be easy. It would have been a lie, and I doubt we would have believed it anyway.

Paulie had suffered a major heart attack and had decided it was time to retire. And, as much as Billy and I liked the money, we had begun to give the retirement idea some serious thought as well. Of course Mary had pretty much convinced Jodie that we now had more than enough money to be able to live comfortably for the rest of our lives, and that there was no need for us to continue fighting. And to be sure, there were much safer ways to make a living. Sadly, Mary was to be proved right on both counts.

While this was an eventful year for us, it wasn't anything earthshaking. And by the time the year ended, Billy and I were still champions of the world.

However, the following year, 1948, almost saw the end of both of Billy's and my ring careers. It also saw the United Nations create the Country of Israel, which, although in the middle of a baron desert, has created a lot of chaos in the Middle East ever since. It was also highlighted by the Marshall Plan that gave aide to our allies, and the assassination, in India of their spiritual leader, Ghandi.

It wasn't that anyone in our family was against the creation of Israel, in truth we could care less. It didn't seem to affect our lives in any way, and besides, they were half a world away. Who knew the problems that would be created? Even after they were immediately attacked by the Arab States, they defended themselves well, won the victory and survived, a trait that many boxers need to learn.

Billy and I decided that instead of hiring a trainer and a cornerman, we'd work instead in each other's corners and not fight on the same card again. We figured that would save us some extra cash for our planned upcoming retirement, although we didn't know for sure when that retirement was going to come. Our plans were simple, when one of us lost the title, we'd both hang up the gloves.

Billy also had filled out and outgrown the welterweight division, and he decided to move up a division to try his luck at middleweight. We knew we would never have to fight each other, because even if Billy was successful, I'd move up a weight class as well, to light heavyweight. I was walking around at about 180 those days anyway.

You see, we didn't have all the weight divisions that we have today. There was no junior or super anything…Just eight weight classes. There was no cruiserweight class at the time either.

A fighter was allowed to keep his belt, so Billy didn't have to give up the welterweight title. He decided not to vacate that belt quite yet. He hadn't fought the bigger punchers, which usually come at the heavier weights, but he had sparred with me in the gym, many times. We both felt he could handle the harder hitters with ease. This was to prove an almost very costly miscalculation.

We did speak to Paulie about it, and he too didn't like the idea of Billy moving to middleweight. "Stay at welterweight! The punchers in the middleweight class are far too big and strong for you, son," Paulie advised him.

Despite Paulie's seemingly sage advice and the many threats on Billy's life, and having a hard time breathing from a prolonged cold he had been trying, but was unable to shake, Billy was to remain stubborn till the end.

Against our advice and better judgment, Billy decided to make the move up to middleweight and was going to make his debut at the higher weight at a fight in Charleston, South Carolina. Billy was to go in against an up and coming black kid, who although not a very big puncher, was very fast and elusive and could fight like the dickens.

This was going to be a truly worthy adversary for Billy. If he lost the fight, he had promised Mary he would retire and give up his welterweight belt, even though that was not required.

This was going to be Billy's last fight, but we had no thought of that at the time.

Taking this fight was clearly Billy's idea. He figured that even if he lost, he couldn't get badly injured, because Sam Moss, the guy he was facing, would wear you down, but couldn't knock you out, even if he used a tranquilizer gun. As the saying went, 'he couldn't break an egg, even if it was half cracked'.

Billy must have also known full well that the many threats he had received in the mail came from racial hate mongers, mainly from the South. He didn't realize how dangerous it could be to taunt them by fighting a black man in their backyard. It simply made no sense, but I didn't know anything about the threats that had been made against Billy at the time. If I did, things could have been a lot different. All I could advise him to do was not to risk losing a hometown decision and to fight closer to home. But Billy always had that stubborn streak in him, and when his mind was made up, he wouldn't listen to me or anyone else.

So, heavy cold or not, Billy certainly had not taken the train all the way to Charleston to lose. He had trained very hard for the fight, harder than I had ever seen him. He had a small fever when we arrived, but Billy had made up his mind and win or lose, this fight was going to happen.

Sam Moss, his opponent, was a true middleweight and a great boxer out of New Orleans. Billy knew full well that he would have his work cut out for him. So did I, and in fact I strongly advised him again against taking this fight. But not because of the death threats. I knew nothing of them at this time.

I told Billy that there were a lot of much easier foes, so why take on a tough, highly ranked customer like Moss in his debut as middleweight? Sure Billy didn't figure to get knocked out, because Moss, although a middleweight, couldn't punch his way out of a paper bag. He won all his fights by wearing down his opponents with body punches and out-boxing them. He would tire them out by making them miss badly early in the fight, and then when that happened he came on like a house on fire to take the later rounds and the decision.

I had advised Billy to work his way up the rankings slowly, by fighting easier competition so he could get used to carrying the extra weight in the ring, before meeting a guy who could fight as well and was as fast as Sam Moss.

Billy simply said, this will be one of his bigger paydays, so even if he lost, it would only be via decision. At worst we'd both be able to retire in style and enjoy our lives in comfort, should we choose to do so.

It was hard to argue with that logic, but if I had only known about the threats, maybe I could have done a lot more to discourage him, or have extra security on hand. But since Billy was so darn stubborn, I'll never know, but I still shoulder some of the blame and guilt to this day, for what was to happen next.

I trained very hard with Billy for this fight, running, tossing the medicine ball, jumping rope, riding the bike, shadow boxing and sparring. Billy, although weak was as sharp as I'd ever seen him, and he seemed able to carry the extra weight without any problems. The question was, would his punch be as lethal against a heavier foe? And what type of toll would his cold take on him? As it happened, it proved to be the heat and humidity as much as his cold that would decide the outcome.

It was a very humid March 15, the Ides of March, with gnats and other bugs flourishing everywhere, when Billy met Sam Moss in the outdoor makeshift ring. Moss was undefeated at the time. He also was a strong body puncher and had caused a half dozen or so of his opponents to quit in their corner. Some of them had suffered broken ribs. But his knockouts were not of the one-punch variety. Moss liked to wear down his foes and then out-box them. In the trade he was called a 'cutey'.

The match was held at a minor league baseball park, with portable wooden bleacher seats set up around the ring. The fight occurred during the heat of the day, which also was an edge for Moss, who, because he was from the South was used to those conditions

The stands were packed and I'd be lying if I didn't hear a lot of folks screaming racist slogans at the top of their lungs. Most seemed to be waving Confederate flags. Didn't they realize the war was over long ago?

I know the crowd wasn't rooting for Billy because they liked him, they were rooting for him because he was white and his opponent was a minority. In truth they were rooting against Sam Moss. It was indeed a sad commentary of those times in the South.

To be honest, hearing those shouts just turned my stomach, and knowing Billy, he didn't like it one bit either, although he never mentioned it to me more than once. What did Sam Moss or any Negro do to anger these bigots anyway?

"I ought to let this Moss guy win, just to shut these damn fucking stupid bigots up", Billy said, as he was loosening up in the corner. "Don't these asshole morons know that black folks bleed the same red blood as we do?" I rarely heard Billy curse before.

Suddenly I took notice and thought it a bit odd, that Bob Harrison who had followed both our careers from ringside since his retirement, wasn't in attendance. Listening to the fans though, it was easy to understand why. He might have been in the crowd, but probably wouldn't have been allowed to sit at ringside no matter how much he paid for a ticket. Hell, they may not have even let him in the arena. As it happened, I found out later that Bob didn't make the trip.

"Don't do it, Billy, I calmly advised. "Win this fight and go out on top so you can continue your career. If you do lose, show some dignity. Give it your all! Don't stoop to the level of these stupid hate-mongers. This guy's got some pounds and a big height and reach advantage on you, so you have to work your way inside to do any serious damage. Don't try to fight him from the outside. That's what he wants you to do. Hit and run, that's your best shot."

Rusty Rubin

But Billy was too weakened by the flu to fight that kind of fight. He nodded silently, I assumed in agreement.

And the fans continued to boo loudly and threw whatever they could find towards Moss' corner, and the din grew even louder when Billy and Sam Moss touched gloves in center ring. I guess, in their twisted minds you couldn't even shake hands with a black man.

I even heard a Southern female waving a rebel flag voice yell, "Go get him, Billy. Kill that mother fucking nigger".

I wanted to vomit. I wanted to be anyplace else in the world but here and now. Not out of fear, but out of disgust for what I was hearing and seeing. Hard to believe we were almost midway through the 20th Century.

The fight was making me sick before it even started. Billy or I should have insisted on taking this match in a Northern City, where he didn't have to deal with such a prejudiced crowd. I thought he took the fight because he didn't realize the hatred that was waiting for him in Charleston. He did, but didn't care. I know that from the hate mail I found later.

It was almost as if Billy was just asking for trouble. Maybe he wanted to prove a point, but to this day, I have no idea what that point was.

The ring was cleared of all the debris and the bell sounded. Immediately Moss started throwing fast, wicked body punches, a bit out of style for him. Billy tried to counter with his jab, but Moss stayed out of range, closing only to throw body shots, with an occasional shot to the head, that Billy easily picked off. Still Moss was landing and Billy wasn't. And the crowd wasn't very happy and let Billy know about it in no uncertain terms.

Billy came back to the corner after the first round, a bit out of breath. He had never faced such a powerful foe and had gone into this bout with no idea what it would be like to face a strong body puncher like Moss. And his head cold certainly wasn't helping him either.

"You gave away that round champ. But we've still got nine more to go, now you have to start working his body to have a chance of picking up some rounds. Forget the right hand for now, the opportunity will be there for you later in the fight." I'm not sure I really believed what I was saying about the opening, but it was sound advice.

Paulie later told me that it was the right advice, and against a less inspired and powerful opponent, should have worked very well. But this was to be Sam Moss' day, and nothing that Billy was able to do was going to change that.

By round five, Billy, who had not won a round, was coughing and wheezing, and although I knew he had a bad cold, the thought occurred to me that he might now also have a broken rib. A malady not uncommon among Moss' opponents.

"You okay, Billy", I asked as he slowly sat on the stool, head down. His face was largely unmarked, but he had large red welts on his stomach and sides, the result of the powerful pounding he was taking to the body.

"I'm not really sure, Tony. I never faced someone this strong. I'm having a hard time catching my breath".

"You want me to throw in the towel?" I asked reaching for the thick piece of cotton. "He's beating the heck out of you. You haven't come close to winning a round yet, and you don't look like you're going to get any better. Is that cold bothering you?"

Billy thought a moment. "I'm sure that it's not helping my breathing any, but the ribs are what's hurting me at the moment. I can't take a deep breath. Don't stop the fight yet. I think I'm tiring him out by letting him throw all those body punches. Give me a couple more rounds. Remember where we're fighting. The judges might be prejudiced and scoring some of these rounds for me."

"You haven't come close to winning a round, yet". I argued.

"OK, Tony, just give me one more round, then".

"You don't want to win on a bad decision, Billy. We both know that. Look, one loss isn't going to kill you", I protested, not realizing the irony my words were to prove. "You still have the welterweight title. You could always drop back down again."

"Can't do it, Tony. I didn't tell you before, but it's too hard for me to make the weight anymore. I'm too big for welterweight and too small for middleweight. Maybe this is going to be the time to just hang em up and enjoy the rest of my life. But I'm not going out without giving it my all. Broken ribs will heal. I'm not a quiter."

Billy would give it his all and then some.

In round six, Billy winced every time Moss landed a body punch, and he did so often. I winced each time, also, knowing the pain my brother must be feeling. I was convinced that he had sustained at least one broken rib and I had no alternative but to throw in the towel.

It was bedlam. Suddenly things were being thrown into the ring, and we had to duck to prevent any damage from being hit. We ducked through the ropes and ran as fast as we could. Billy was gasping for air all he way. He wasn't able to run very fast at that point. A bottle hit him on his lower back as we reached the safety of the dugout and then the dressing room. The security guards had their hands full trying to control the crowd. A few even got through, and we heard the kicking and banging on our dressing room door, before they were subdued.

Sam Moss had almost the same problem, and we were very glad to find out that he had made it back to the safety of his dressing room as well.

Arriving in our dressing room in one piece, we took a deep breath, and Billy was coughing and tears were in his eyes. He was clearly in a lot of pain. I wanted to call an ambulance and get him to a hospital, but he wanted to act like a tough a guy and didn't trust the doctors in Charleston, anyway.

This just wasn't our kind of town. Although, looking back, maybe calling the ambulance would have been a much better and safer move.

We knew that the angry crowd was going to be hanging around awhile to curse and throw some more things at us. We also knew it wasn't Billy's fault and that he had given it his best shot, which is all that should be expected of any fighter. The crowd may have expected it, but they sure didn't accept it gracefully.

The angry fans either didn't want to know or care. Billy was drained from the head cold as well as from the beating he had just taken, but Billy would never make excuses. "I was beaten by a better man today", he told the assembled press after things had died down. "I was beaten badly by one of the best middleweights around. I take my hat off to Sam Moss."

"Right now I don't know if I want a rematch or not," he continued. "I just want to go back to Philly and spend some time with my family, before I decide what my next move will be."

We were very shocked to learn that Billy was ahead on the judges scorecards when we stopped the fight. It made us wonder how a black man could ever win a match in the South. I figured the only way that would happen is if he fought another black man.

When asked again if he wanted a rematch, Billy looked at me and said to the press. "It's Sam's call. If he wants to give me a rematch, Tony and I will talk it over and we'll have an announcement when we make up our minds. Right now, I don't think I ever want to step into the same ring with him again. He's a future champion, no doubt about it!"

The reporters turned to me, "if we do fight him again, it will be in Philadelphia," I said. "This type of crowd gives me the creeps. How could people be so ignorant? Billy may also drop back to welterweight, where he still holds the title. Or he may just decide to retire. We'll wait and see."

"Would you fight Moss to avenge your brother's loss?" a reporter asked.

"I honestly haven't given it any thought". I replied. "I guess that's possible. Right now we have to take Billy to the hospital".

We showered and quietly waited around for a few hours before leaving to make sure the crowd had disbanded. Billy had called home, and Mary sounded hysterical on the phone. Someone with a deep southern accent had called their house and had threatened to kill him. It was the first and only time she had found out about the death threats. To be safe she notified the authorities in Philadelphia and in Charleston.

"Don't worry, Sweetheart", Billy said. "It's just another empty threat from one of these racist whacko's. I'll be fine."

I'm not sure what Mary said on the other end, but Billy laughed, clutching his ribs. "Call the State police? For what? A stupid phone call? It's just some harmless nut. Talk is cheap! Tony and I will grab the train and be home tomorrow afternoon. Relax. Love ya"

Billy saw the confused look on my face and smiled. "Just another stupid bigot who didn't like the outcome of the fight. I don't worry about these guys. They call or write nasty letters all the time. If they want to get you, they don't call and tell you to look out for them. It's the ones that don't make the threats that you have to be on the lookout for. Mary wants me to call the State Troopers here. I haven't seen any black ones around, have you? Do you really think they would lift a finger to protect me?"

It made sense to me and we never called the State Police, just the local authorities. It was another big mistake.

After the security guards cleared the stadium, we called a cab to take us to the hospital but changed our mind and went to our hotel instead. That turned out to be the worst choice we could have made. But we knew that the next morning we would be all packed and heading for the train to take us home. Billy said he would go to the hospital in Philadelphia to have his ribs taped before returning home.

The taxi ride was uneventful and there was little conversation. We were actually feeling relief that the burden was now off us. We would never fight in the South again and we would probably announce our retirement when we got home and talked it over with our wives, who we knew would be very happy to learn about our decision.

I also seriously thought of giving Moss a shot at my middleweight belt, and avenging Billy's defeat. But I didn't mention that to Billy.

When we got out of the cab, carrying our gear slowly walked towards our hotel entrance, I heard a loud cracking sound, and suddenly Billy fell to the ground clutching his chest. He had been shot from one of the rooftops across the street. A second bullet then whizzed by my head and shattered the glass on the revolving door of the hotel.

The shooter must have fled, because fortunately there was no third bullet, and I didn't think of running for cover. I kneeled by Billy's side, blocking the snipers angle, not thinking of my own safety, just wanting to make sure that another shot didn't hit him. The hotel doorman quickly called the police and an ambulance, which arrived a bit slower than I would have liked. I won't make any accusations here, because under the circumstances, time was crawling by and the life was seeping out of my brother.

All I could do is cover his wound and watching Billy, face down on the cold sidewalk, bleeding, his life ebbing away, every minute seemed like an eternity to me.

I heard sirens and I knew help was on the way and I prayed with all my might that they were not going to be too late.

A large crowd had gathered around, including a couple of reporters, and photographers, but I hardly took notice of them. They had the good sense to know that this was not a good time to ask any questions. I put my satchel under Billy's head, and when I saw that there was also some blood coming out of the corner of his mouth. I knew that he was in very bad shape. Worse than I dared imagine.

The ambulance arrived and I rode in it with Billy, to the hospital. They medics gave him first aide, but by the look on their faces, I knew this was Billy's final moments on this earth. On the way to the emergency room, he opened his eyes and said "Tony, please take care of Mary and Billy Jr." He hesitated, and reached out and touched my hand "and please help him become a boxer, if that's what he wants to do. It's an honorable and honest profession." I took hold of his shoulder, and though the tears were welling up in my eyes and inside me, I made him that promise. "And Tony, you don't have to retire if you really don't want to". Those were Billy's last words. He lapsed into a coma.

Billy was dead by the time they reached the emergency room, and although they tried their best to revive him, he had lost too much blood. He was just 23, although his obituary read 25, because that's what we told the promoters. The secret would remain safe with me, until now. I called a church and had a priest come to give him the last rites.

I could have used some emotional help from the priest, but didn't think of asking for it. I was beside myself. I was crying, I was angry, I was experiencing just about every emotion there was and then some. Why did this have to happen? Why Billy? Why not me? I started feeling guilty that I wasn't the victim instead. Billy had a family, so did I, but. I had lived two years longer than him, why couldn't it be me?

I knew it wasn't a logical question. I knew Billy was killed because he happened to be the one who lost to a black fighter, not me, although I was the one who threw in the towel. Besides, didn't the killer try to take me out as well? I knew that I had to get back in full control of my emotions. I knew it wasn't the fault of boxing, but rather some hateful jerk that didn't understand that all men were created equal. I would have given my right arm to find him and just have two minutes alone, just that bastard and myself. But that too was just another wasted emotion.

I knew that Mary was going to be beside herself, and except for Jodie and Paulie, I had nowhere left to turn.

Aunt Jen, bless her soul, had lost her mind, I guess you'd call it Alzheimer's today, and was now living out her final days in a nursing home. She didn't know any of the family most of the time, even when we visited, which at first was very often. She wouldn't last out the year.

Then, in a more lucid moment, I realized that I had to call Mary. I knew it wouldn't be easy breaking the news to her. Instead I called Jodie, who I felt would be able to break the news to Billy's widow in a much softer manner. I was crying when I called home.

Mary was in our apartment with Jodie, and she had already heard the tragic news on the radio, and was hysterical.

And Jodie told me that the phones were ringing constantly with reporters asking their stupid, insensitive questions. Why couldn't they wait for me to return? The police and the FBI were also on hand to investigate. I told Jodie to tell Mary not to answer any questions and that I would be taking Billy's body home with me, and to tell the police and the press I'd speak with them the next day.

When I returned home, Mary's attitude was very bitter, she felt that if it weren't for boxing, Billy would still be alive. She didn't give credit to the sport that got her the new home, and paid for a lifestyle that she probably would never have ever had otherwise. Although I think everyone knew that we'd rather have Billy back and live in poverty if necessary. But trying to reason with Mary at that moment in time was only going to make matters worse.

I knew the truth was going to be very hard for her to accept. It wasn't the sport of boxing that killed Billy, but an out of his mind, racist, who was going to get paid back, hopefully by me.

When I returned home, after making sure Billy's casket was dropped at the funeral home, Jodie was holding Mary while tears welled in both their eyes. I felt both guilty and helpless at the same time. There was little I could say or do. I was still wearing my shirt that was stained with the blood of my now deceased brother, and of course wished that I had the common sense to have changed it.

I had other mixed feelings as well, and my heart was beating faster than I could ever remember. I know that we had promised Mary and Jodie that when one of us lost, it would be our last fight. But it all was very different

243

now. I didn't want to quit on a losing note, and let everyone think the Petrovic brothers were quitters. I wasn't going to let that happen.

More to the point, if I quit, then these bastards that had killed my brother would become the winners. I also now had three more mouths to feed, as Tony Jr. was born a month earlier. I just didn't know what I was going to do. I wanted a match with Sam Moss as badly as I ever wanted a fight. That insensitive reporter in the dressing room was right, Billy had to be avenged.

But I also knew that it wasn't Sam Moss that had killed Billy. I had to keep that in mind as well. Moss had taken the same risk as Billy did, and he almost got killed for it as well.

I showered and finally changed my shirt, and after a long session with the rest of the family, I decided that now we needed the money more than ever, and that I had to continue fighting for at least another year. Jodie understood, Mary didn't, but as much as I cared for Mary, I had to do what was right for Billy and take care of the rest of the family.

"Look what fighting did for Billy. It got him killed. I don't want to lose you too, Tony. You and Jodie are now the only family Billy Jr. and I have left," Mary said.

"And that's exactly the reason, why I have to fight on." I explained. "At least for one more year. Now I have two more mouths to feed, and…"

"I can get a job, and Jodie can watch little Billy and Tony (who was born a Month earlier), or we both can work and we can get a nanny". Mary sobbed.

"The babies need their mother with them, Mary. I know that you mean well. Don't worry, I'll be just fine." I hugged her and kissed the tears that were flowing down her cheeks. She grabbed me tightly and squeezed hard. She needed someone strong to hold onto now. I knew that as helpless as I felt, I had to be that person.

Jodie was silent the entire time. I never knew what she was thinking, but I did know that whatever decision I made, she would completely support it. I really loved her. She was the best wife anyone could ever have.

Then I had to deal with the press. I lied when I told them that I had promised Billy that I would continue fighting, and that's what I was going to do. And if Sam Moss wanted my middleweight title, I'll gladly fight him, but I would never fight him or anyone else again in the South."

But before I made a move, I wanted to call Paulie and see if he had any suggestions. Of course he had heard the news and had immediately called Mary and Jodie with his condolences. I think he was waiting for my call.

"Paulie, this is Tony" I said.

"Tony, I'm so sorry about Billy. He was a great kid. If there's anything I can do…."

"There is! I want to keep on fighting and now I'm in need of a trainer again. You're the only one I have confidence in. Will you work with me again?"

Paulie hesitated. "You know that I'm retired now, Tony. I've got a bad ticker".

"I know, Paulie. Look, let me come over to your place and we'll talk. If nothing else I'm sure you can help me find a new trainer."

He hesitated. "Okay", he sighed. "Come on over."

When I arrived at Paulie's house, I was amazed at how much he seemed to have aged. I figured that he couldn't have been more than sixty, but he now looked about eighty to me. He had lost weight and had wrinkles all over his face. His house was a mess and smelled from stale tobacco and booze. He offered me a drink, which I refused. I smelled liquor on his breath as he poured himself another shot.

"You know you shouldn't be drinking like this, Paulie. It's not good for you."

I noticed that he was still wearing his sweat stained shirt that he always wore in the gym. I couldn't help but wonder if he owned any other clothes. Even the apartment was sparsely furnished and none of the furniture seemed to match. It was obvious that Paulie was down on his luck and was close to giving up.

"Are you gambling again, Paulie?"

"What da hell else do I have to do with the time and money I have left? I've been on a losing streak, but what difference does it make now, Tony. I'm on my last legs anyway. Don't worry, I don't owe any money. If you need some to get by, I'll give ya what's left and stop gambling. Ya didn't come over to discuss my health or my gambling problem, ya wanted me to put you in contact with a new trainer?"

I wasn't sure that Paulie had really stopped gambling. Like drinking and smoking, it's a habit, and Paulie had a lot of them. "Not exactly, Paulie, I said. I still want you for my trainer. One of the things you and boxing have taught me in my lifetime is loyalty."

"Do ya remember that time when I bet against ya and tried to make ya lose?"

"Forget it! That's in the past. Mistakes happen. I need you in my corner, Paulie."

Paulie poured a second drink into a dirty shot glass and handed it to me. "Let's have one drink in memory of Billy Petrovic, a really great champion", he said.

I thought a moment. How could I not drink to that? Paulie always could find my weak spots as well as my strengths.

I wasn't much of a drinker, but downed the whiskey, quickly, feeling a warm surge within. I knew that a lot of ex-fighters were winding up like Paulie, drunk and broke, and I didn't want that to be my legacy to my late younger brother or our families.

"Look Paulie, I just want to fight on for one more year. I want to make enough money to take care of Billy's family and mine. But I need your help. You can come back as a favor to me, just for one year, maybe less. You owe me that much."

Paulie quickly downed his drink.

"Owe ya? Now ya gonna throw that up in my face? I paid ya back all dat fuckin money, I borrowed." He quickly calmed down "Look, I'm really flattered that ya ask, Tony. But just take a look at me. I'm nothing more than an old sot. I can't help ya or anyone else anymore. My career in boxing, like my life, is over, dead, finished. Nobody in their right mind would want an old drunk with a heart condition ter train dem."

"Damn it, stop feeling sorry for yourself, Paulie! I just lost my 23 year old brother, so I'm not in my right mind, now." Paulie just bowed his head. "Are you telling me that you no longer like to feel the excitement, hear the roar of the crowd? I know you a lot better than that, Paulie. I'm asking you to give me one year, no more. If I lose before that time, I'll hang em up and then you can go back to gambling, drinking or whatever you want to do. I need you in my corner and by the looks of this place, you can sure use the money. If not for me, do it for Billy. You got him to the top, remember?"

I must have struck a nerve. I think I saw some tears well up in Paulie's eyes. "Ya really mean that, don't ya Tony? Yer a real champion. What the hell do you need an over the hill drunk like me for?"

Because you brought me to the top. You were with me when I started my career, you were with me when I won the title, and I want you with me when I end it. It's just for one year, Paulie, just a few fights."

Paulie put down his drink, and embraced me. He smelled from a combination of alcohol and sweat. "Tony, ya just gave a stupid old man somethin to live for. Be in the gym on Sunday morning and be ready to work." There was a more than a hint of tears welling up in Paulie's eyes.

"Now you have to do one more thing for me, Paulie. Get rid of the damn bottle. No more drinking you hear, at least until I decide to hang em up."

Paulie nodded and hesitated, then poured what little remained of the bottle down the sink and tossed the bottle in the trash. I swear I saw tears well-up in his eyes when he did so. a I had to wonder if that was because of the wasted booze or because of my trust in him.

I knew that I was taking a big chance with Paulie. I knew about his heart problems and I certainly didn't need his death on my conscience also. Because of his gambling debts he had almost sold Billy and I down the river before, and I knew that he still made bets. But I genuinely liked the guy, and I knew he was a smart, ring-wise trainer. And he, more than anyone else, could help me go out on top. I really did owe him, big!

But first, I had to make the arrangements for Billy's funeral, and that too, I knew was not going to be an easy task.

Chapter VIII

Billy's funeral was held on Aug. 23, and it was very well attended. I was a bit surprised, but pleased that Bob Harrison came by with his wife Jeanette, to offer their sympathy. I was even more surprised when Sam Moss showed up, having taken the train all the way to Philadelphia from his home in New Orleans.

Now that was really a show of class, I thought. Sam shook my hand and expressed his condolences, then walked over and gave Billy's immediate family a big hug and told them how sorry he was. He in a way, felt responsible for Billy's tragic death. I grasped his hand tightly and told him that he had taken his chances as well. I thank God that he wasn't killed also. In truth, with all that bigotry I was surprised that he wasn't the one who was targeted. If it was him instead of Billy who was shot, would we have acted with as much class? I'd like to think so, but we'll never know.

I guess if anything good came out of Billy's death it was that Mary finally admitted that boxing folks were really great guys and boxing was a great fraternity.

We all wept together as one, which I suppose was as it should be.

1949: was also to be my last year as a professional prizefighter. But after Billy's death, I now needed, not only the extra money, but also a way to get Billy's death out of my mind. The sight of him lying outside the hotel, that fateful day, with the life seeping out of him, is something I will never forget. I guess some of the guilt I felt is still with me and always will be. In any event I was going to make darn sure to keep my promise to Billy that Mary and Billy Jr. were always going to be very well provided for.

I suppose that I probably would have continued fighting, even without the promise I had made to Billy. No one really ever knows what he would do until they are actually confronted with a specific situation.

Along with Billy's family, I also had to provide for Jodie and Tony Jr. who was growing very quickly, although still in diapers. I knew he was going to be a big guy when he grew up.

This was also the year that the Communists took over China with the Nationalist Chinese fleeing and setting up a government in exile on Formosa, two islands off the East coast of China. It was also the year that NATO, the North Atlantic Treaty Organization was established. In boxing, Ezzard Charles beat Jersey Joe Walcott to win the heavyweight championship of the world. Charles was one of the best heavyweights of my era, next to Joe Louis of course. The "Brown Bomber" fought a little before my time.

I had taken two non-title bouts early in the spring, which I won easily. But I was obviously now on a head-on collision course with Sam Moss, who also continued to win. He had now become the number one middleweight contender. Because Sam attended the funeral, which was a very decent thing to do, I wasn't completely sure that I really wanted to fight him. But one way or the other, I felt that Billy had to be avenged. The honor of the Petrovic family was at stake.

So against Paulie's sage advice, I took the title fight with this outstanding body-puncher that had given my brother Billy his second defeat. But both Sam and I made darn sure that the fight was going to be held up North, in Scranton, Pennsylvania, a fairly neutral city. The date of the fight was June 24th. It was a fight I now badly wanted, not to hurt Sam, but to protect Billy's image in the mind of his family, fans and friends.

"If yer gonna to take this fight, Tony" Paulie said, "ya gatta build up those stomach muscles. You saw what that Moss kid did to Billy. He's a murderous body puncher."

I nodded and the training regimen that I took to fight Moss now consisted of a lot of extra sit-ups and the frequent use of a 'medicine ball', something I don't believe they use in training today. Paulie wanted to build up my stomach muscles to absorb Moss's power. I also did a lot of extra sparring and running. I wanted to keep my title but I also wanted to avenge Billy, not his death, but his loss.

Although I was only 26, all the extra training I was doing seemed to be taking a bit of a toll on my body, particularly my legs. Maybe it was all the fights I had previously or maybe because I constantly pushed myself too hard. I learned from Paulie that you have to work constantly to be the best, and stay in shape in between fights. That meant no sex. That's one of the problems with many of the fighters of today, they let themselves get out of shape in between fights, and many seem to train on sex.

There is a much bigger gap between fights today than there was when I was fighting. In my day we'd fight 10 times or more a year. Today three or four seems to be the maximum that anyone wants to fight. Of course with the amount of money they make today, you can't really blame them.

I knew in my heart that Sam Moss had absolutely nothing to do with Billy's murder. I harbored no ill well towards him. He was just an outstanding fighter that did his job and did it well. Sam Moss also had risked his life that fateful day in Charleston.

I liked and respected him for the class he showed by coming to Billy's funeral. As I recall he asked for me before he came up to make sure that it was okay for a black man to attend a white funeral. Such were the times. I suppose if Billy's funeral was held in the South, no black man would be allowed to pay their respects. The days after Billy's death remain a blur to this day.

Sam wasn't the only black person at Billy's funeral. Billy had earned the respect and friendship of many others, including Bob Harrison and his wife, who I know were at the wake and funeral.

But I also knew that I wanted to beat Moss decisively to avenge my kid brother. My only concern was that I wouldn't overdo it, because having one ring death on my conscience (George Schultz) was much more than enough to retire with. I just wanted to show Moss and the world that the Petrovic family was going out on top, as winners. Yet, I also realized that Moss was a great competitor and if I held back too much, I could lose the fight.

It's tough to have to look at both sides of a boxing match like that. On one hand you want to win and avenge your brother, on the other, you really like and respect your opponent and don't want to hurt him. Talk about being in a quandary. But I was a professional boxer, and proud of my family name, and I knew in my heart what I had to do. I just wanted to do it with a decision, and then retire.

Shortly after Billy's funeral, Bob Harrison called the house to again express his sympathy. He asked me if he could help out in any way, to let him know. I told him that I was looking for some extra sparring, as it would be a major health risk for Paulie to put on the big mitts and work out with me and somebody had to. Harrison readily volunteered. I knew that he would.

I knew he would never approve, so without Paulie's direct knowledge, Harrison and I set up a ring and sparred in the backyard of our house. Paulie was always worried that I would over-train, but I remember that he also told me to 'listen to my body'. If it says enough, it's enough. While working out in the gym and the yard, my body would refuse to say 'enough'.

Sure, at night I felt like all the muscles in my body was cramping and throbbing, and I almost felt like retiring at that time. Jodie sensed the pain I was in and asked me to call it a career. But I could never go out a quitter. That wasn't my nature. The Petrovic family honor was at stake, at least in my mind.

Paulie also had me working out against some of the other guys in the gym. He had them holding the big mitts and moving side to side, so Paulie could watch from the ring apron and didn't have to over-exert himself. Paulie would always stand below the ring, an unlit cigar in his mouth and looking up and yelling out directions to me. I think his favorite word was "again."

But in the end, even the extra steps I had taken to protect Paulie didn't matter. Three weeks before the title fight, Paulie suffered another heart attack at his home, and he was now pretty much confined to the house. I told him that I'd postpone the Moss fight till he got better, but he just shook his head. "Forget it Tony. We both know I'm finished and that I'll never get any better, Tony. Even though I can't be there, I'll be listening on the radio and rooting for you. Heck, except for Billy's funeral service, I haven't been to a church in years, but I'll be praying for you too".

Then I told Paulie that although I'd now have to find another trainer, he would still get his cut of my purse. I wasn't fighting this fight for the money or the fame, just for Billy and his family.

"Ya don't have ta do dat, Tony. I've made quite a few winning bets lately. I can manage. Besides, we both know I can't take it with me, and you, Jodie. Billy and Mary are the only family I've had in years".

He may have been lying about his winning bets, but I didn't know what to say to him. I was crying like a baby. The doctor had told me that Paulie had less than a year to live. He probably had told Paulie the same thing. Paulie obviously knew that the end was near.

"Paulie", I said, "it's not only the right thing to do, it's what I want to do. At least it will help pay for your medical bills. You have to know that Billy would have wanted it that way also."

Paulie shook his head. "Tony, when I'm gone, there's no one left dat da bookies can go after to pay what I might owe them. I have no family, you do. Keep all the money for them. Send Tony Jr. to college on a "Paulie Scholarship". College is the way of the future. Boxing is too dangerous, and much too corrupt. At every turn, it keeps shooting itself in the foot."

I wasn't going to argue with an old friend on his deathbed. I had already made up my mind that I was going to cover all of Paulie's medical expenses as well as his funeral when he passed on. If needed, the bookies would be paid off too. I wanted Paulie to go out of this world the way he came into it, with a clean slate. He deserved that much. I quickly changed the subject.

"Do you have any suggestions as to who should be training me? I asked. "It's going to be my last fight and I intend to go out on top."

Paulie then mentioned the names of a couple of long time gym rats that he felt could give me the training I needed, and help guide me through this fight. But Paulie named no one I felt very comfortable with. These guys had never trained anyone. They knew little about giving the right advice, and really weren't even good sparring partners. Without Paulie and Billy around, I knew I had to find the right person to handle me, or my title would be gone. I had promised Jodie and Mary, that this was the end of my boxing career.

"Paulie's on his last legs and he's not going to make it. Now I have to find the right trainer to take over", I told Bob Harrison, toweling myself off after a long, sweaty sparring session in the backyard.

He toweled himself off also. "Look no further, Tony. That is if you don't mind being managed and trained by a black man, who has never trained anyone else before."

"What about your regular job in the defense plant?" I asked. "I need full time training till the fight and I don't think you can't afford to lose your job."

"Hey, Tony, where've you been? The war has been over for some time now. The defense plant closed down last year. I've been working as an insurance salesman for the past few years. And that job allows me more than enough time to work my own hours. Jeanette likes you and Mary and certainly wont mind. It won't be a problem financially, I promise. In fact, if you want to help out, take out a life insurance policy. I have some good ones to offer. I wish I was selling this stuff before Billy's last fight. He would have left some good money to Mary."

Jeanette was Bob's wife, whom I had met on a few occasions in the past, the last time being at Billy's funeral.

Why didn't I think about Harrison training me? Bob and his wife had become very good friends, I think that of all the people I knew I could confide in and trust, Bob and Jeanette were special. I never really noticed or cared about the color of his, or anyone else's skin. He was a great guy and a true friend, and he could be trusted. And he knew the fight game, and that was all that really mattered.

But before I agreed to let Bob train me, I made it very clear that I didn't want to resort to using dirty tactics, like he used to do, to beat Moss. And I also made him happy by taking out a $50,000 policy on my life.

Harrison shrugged, then grinned. "If you want a clean fight, that's your call, Tony. I was taught to do whatever you have to do to win, that is as long as the ref wasn't looking." He chuckled. "But Sam Moss is far from a dirty fighter, he's damn good and he knows it. He knows down deep that he doesn't have to fight dirty to win. As far as I know he never has. He has more natural ability than most of the pugs around."

"Bob", I responded. "You know that I only stooped to that level in that one fight against you. And you're the one who started it. I don't like fighting dirty and I don't want to stoop to that level again. If it means losing to Moss, so be it."

"Can't argue with you there, Tony. But I really feel that if you get the opportunity to do some serious damage without the ref seeing, you should take it. Accidental low blows often happen in the heat of the action. And if it gives you the edge…" His voice trailed off, "But that's your call. I won't press the issue."

"It's just not my style, Bob" I grinned. "Never has been. I want to win this fight badly and to keep my title, but I don't want it badly enough to have to resort to anything illegal. If I lose, so be it. I want to go out on top, knowing that I gave it my best shot. Billy would have wanted it that way. Besides Moss is a class act."

When I told Paulie about my decision, he expressed his doubts. "Harrison's a damn nice guy, but he never trained anyone before. Ya gonna need someone with far more experience than him. These guys at the gym that I recommended to ya, they've had more than their share of fights and have worked a few corners as well. Besides, the crowd may go against you with a black guy working ya corner."

"But those gym guys were all losers", I responded. "Just look at their records. Harrison went out on top, with a win and a fine winning record. And I don't give a rat's ass how any stupid bigots may feel."

"Look, Tony, ta tell ya da honest truth, I think dat all Bob Harrison knows how to do is ta fight dirty. That's why he hadda winning record. He cheated. He can't teach you anything that these guys in the gym can't."

I shook my head. "Sorry, Paulie, I love and respect you, but my mind is made up. Harrison knows that I intend to fight a clean fight and that he has to train me to win that way".

Paulie shrugged. "Do ya really think dat he can? It's your call. Remember, that with a black trainer ya might be setting yourself up for another nut job to go after you. And dat would really devastate ya family".

This conversation made me wonder if Paulie himself might be a bit or a racist, but I think I knew him well enough to let that ugly thought pass. Paulie knew me well enough to know that once I made my mind up, arguing would be futile. He wished me the best of luck. He told me I'd be in his prayers, and I gave him a big hug and left.

I still had a major problem. While Paulie was running the gym, Harrison was allowed to come up and visit and watch me work out. But the new owners of the gym were very prejudiced and said there was no way they'd allow a black guy to walk into the gym, let alone train me there. In that gym, black fighters and trainers were persona non grata. They were not welcome.

I couldn't believe all their stupidity, but aside from calling them a few choice names before I left, they did own the gym and there was nothing much I could do about it. I know Paulie probably needed the money badly, but it was obvious that he could have made a far better choice to whom he sold the gym.

But I also made a decision. I was never going to set foot in that gym again as long as those narrow minded, racist assholes owned it. I quickly cleaned out my locker and left, leaving them a parting shot.

"As bad as it was, this gym smelled a hell of a lot better when Paulie was running it".

I called Paulie, to tell him about the jerks he had sold the gym to. All he said was "I agree with you, and I wish that I could be ah help, Tony. These guys made me the best offer, and dey paid it all in cold hard cash. It's not my gym no longer. I don't have any juice with the new owners. I figured they'd turn out to be fuckin assholes, but it's their gym now, and their call."

Bob Harrison was obviously used to being treated as a second class citizen, (if one, in truth, can ever get used to it, I know I couldn't). I decided that we'd work outdoors in the backyard in the good weather and indoors, by setting up a ring in his basement when the weather wouldn't cooperate.

But for the most part, the weather was great and Harrison, Jeanette and I really found a bond together. I was almost 27, and he was my first real friend. Bob and his wife had become most welcome guests in our home at lunch or dinnertime. We also shared many meals in their home as well.

The three weeks of heavy training went by fast and well. I was sharp and eager to avenge Billy's loss.

Sam Moss had arrived it town the day before the big fight and called me to tell me again how sorry he was about Billy's death. It was a classy thing to do, but why hadn't he called me when he heard that Billy had been shot? Then again, I thought, maybe he did. I don't have a lot of memories of the week or two after Billy was killed, and certainly no good ones, The phone did ring constantly and we got a lot of sympathy cards. It was total chaos.

Sam took the time and money out of his own pocket to come to Billy's funeral. How could I think ill of him? I couldn't and didn't. He also thanked me for giving him a shot at my title.

In any case, I knew that it was a very kind and sincere gesture on his part. I thanked him for the call and wished him well in our fight.

Before he hung up, he said, "I also want to wish you luck in the fight, Tony. May the best man win."

"You must have heard that Bob Harrison is now training me." I laughed. "Don't worry, Sam, there will be nothing illegal on my part," I said.

Sam laughed loudly. "Bob's a good guy, you're lucky to have him in your corner. I know you're not a dirty fighter, Tony. I'm not at all worried about that".

I thanked him again, and hung up.

I wondered if this was a ploy to quench my anger in case I was still angry over Billy's death, or was the wish genuine? I knew I wouldn't find out till we met in the ring the next night. But I never harbored any hard feelings towards Sam Moss. He had beaten Billy fair and square.

The fight had been switched from Scranton, where it was at first scheduled to be held. It was to take place in Connie Mack Stadium in Philadelphia, a Major League baseball park that had lights for night games, which most pro ballparks had by this time. Lots of extra seats were added all around the ring to accommodate the anticipated large crowd, and the press contingent at ringside.

In the dressing room, Bob Harrison wrapped my hands, put on the gloves and gave me my final instructions.

"Tony, I want you to listen to me very carefully. You know that this guy is a solid body puncher, so you have to fight just like I taught you, from a crouch, elbows in tight so you can protect those ribs. I'm sure that he knows that you have never liked to fight from a crouch before, so he won't expect that and we'll have the element of surprise working in our favor."

During training, I had heard Bob say that more times than I'd care to count, and I had worked from a crouch constantly during that training. It was a brand new style for me, and frankly not a very comfortable one. But I trusted Harrison and what he told me to do seemed to make all the sense in the world. Why wouldn't it? He was a not only my trainer, he had become my best friend.

I was the world champion and the crowd favorite, so I allowed Moss to be the first fighter in the ring, to a loud chorus of boos. Because of what happened to Billy, I was hoping that the boos were more for me, and not because Sam Moss was black.

Letting your opponent go into the ring first, then let him cool off while waiting for you was a head game, still used by many trainers today. "Make your opponent stand in the ring, get nervous and cool down while he waits for you", was Bob Harrison's advice."

Moss had seen it all, so I really doubted that tactic would work, but as Bob said, anything to make this fight easier and safer is worth the shot."

After a few minutes, I followed Sam down the long corridor, to the ring, with Bob Harrison walking alongside me, holding the spit bucket and my mouthpiece. He was also going to be my only cornerman this evening. I figured that win or lose; he could use the extra money. And he sure as hell deserved it.

The referee, a heavy, balding, short guy who obviously couldn't move very fast, called us to ring center and told us, pro forma, that he wanted a clean fight, and what moves he would or would not allow. There was no stare-down and we wished each other luck by touching gloves.

Moss was tall and rangy, but so was I. There was very little difference in our height and weight, although he probably had a small reach advantage, and I had the heavier muscles. I knew he had the hand and foot speed and could and would body punch till the cows came home. I hoped the cows would arrive early.

I couldn't help but think that with Harrison as my trainer, and despite our phone conversation, Moss would still expect me to use illegal tactics.

The bell rang and we touched gloves again, and spent most of the first round circling each other, trying to figure what the other fighter was going to do. There was very little action and the crowd loudly voiced their displeasure in a chorus of boos.

But, I never heard any racial slurs, which made me happy that I was fighting Moss in the Northeast and not in the South.

As the fight went on, Moss would throw body punches, which were picked off by my arms and elbows, and I'd be lying if I said they didn't sting. I knew that I'd be black and blue for a week or more after this fight.

Rusty Rubin

I'd respond with some short uppercuts and combinations, and used my jab to try to keep him off me. Although I had trained that way, I didn't feel at all comfortable fighting from the crouch position.

It went on this way for six rounds. Moss was clearly throwing the most punches, but I was landing more to the vital areas, and landing heavier blows as well. But neither Harrison nor myself had any idea how the scoring was going.

Obviously if it ended at this point, the scorecards were going to be very close.

At least this new crouching style had kept my ribs pretty much intact.

The crowd, wanting to see a lot more action (I must admit that in this mode of fighting, it was hard if not impossible to let go with the big KO punch). Their boos let both Moss and me know about it, big time.

In round seven, Moss changed his tactics and started head hunting, probably trying to please the crowd and impress the judges. He knew that most of his body shots weren't landing anyway. I wasn't prepared for this change in tactics and took a few extra shots to the face than before. There was no question that Moss had won that round, and although I may have been the local favorite, that this was still a very close fight.

I went back to my corner and sat down. "You okay, Tony?" Harrison asked, pouring water over my head. "I don't see any blood".

"I'm fine, Bob. But what do you want me to do now? Do I stay in the crouch and let him play my face like a drum, or should I go back to my normal style of fighting?" At this juncture I almost wished that I had followed Paulie's sage advice and gotten a more experienced trainer.

"Start out in the crouch, but when he throws his first punch towards your head, lean into him with your shoulders and block it, straighten up quick, get on the inside, force him to the ropes and bang away. This fight is way too close to leave up to the judges. To be safe, you have to win just about every round from here on out. Go out there and prove who the real champion is."

I took Harrison's advice in round eight, but Moss wasn't about to let himself get trapped in the corners or on the ropes. He was too strong, too smart and too fast for that. I probably landed enough solid punches to win that round, but it was another close one that the judges easily could have scored either way.

But the crowd roar indicated that they seemed to think that they now were getting their money's worth.

The good news for me was that in those days, you 'had to take the title from the champion'; you couldn't fight close rounds to outpoint him because the judges tended to give all those close rounds to the champ. In short, Moss had to beat me decisively to take the title, and I knew that if I could just limit his body shots for the rest of the bout, he wouldn't be able to do it.

The action slowed during, next three rounds, but were also very close. Again the crowd was not happy with the action, or lack of, and let us know about it. What they had expected to be an exciting bout was turning out to be a dull one.

Round 12 proved to be the pivotal round.

Harrison told me between rounds, that I was doing okay. I was taking away Moss' fight plan since he wasn't doing much damage to my ribs, and that it had to be very frustrating for Moss. He also suggested it may be time for a strategic low blow, but I told him that wasn't going to happen.

Of course it was easy for Bob to say, he wasn't taking any of the punishment. But I knew that I was at least holding my own and I also knew that almost every round could have been scored either way.

In round 12, Moss started out by nailing me with some powerful and painful body shots. He had me against the ropes, in my corner, and just kept pounding away at my body. I was having a hard time catching my breath and blocking this onslaught was certainly not an easy task. I hardly had the energy left to respond. I needed my second wind. So this is what Billy felt like, I thought, fleetingly.

But Billy had fought in the heat and humidity with a bad head cold and a weight disadvantage, and if he could do it, so could I. Of course Billy was a lot faster than I could ever dream of being.

It was then that juncture that Harrison gave me that extra motivation, as he yelled; "Uppercut, Tony! Uppercut! You've got to win this one for Billy, champ!"

I was so engrossed in this close title defense and the battering I was taking blows against the ropes. I had forgotten for a moment about avenging Billy. I got angry, and with a big boost of adrenaline, I threw the uppercut that landed flush. I turned Moss around, and with his back against the ring post. I started banging away at him from side to side, head to body, landing most of my punches. I wasn't going to let this fight go the full 15 rounds.

Moss was a spent fighter and didn't have enough energy left to fight back. His legs sagged. Why wasn't the ref stopping the fight? Was this like my fight with Schultz all over again?

I heard Harrison yelling at the top of his lungs, "You got him, Tony! Win it for Billy. Win it for Billy."

Rusty Rubin

I became very angry now, probably angry enough to do to Moss what I had done to Schultz, but fortunately, the referee wisely finally jumped between us, protecting Moss, and signaled with a waving of his arms that the fight was over.

Bob Harrison was beside himself, tears flowing freely from his eyes. He had never trained a fighter before, let alone a world champion. Sam Moss sat dejectedly on a stool in his corner. I went over to him and congratulated him on a great fight. He smiled and simply said, "I was beaten by a better man tonight. I'll be back."

"You got the rematch whenever you want it, Sam. You fought a great fight. You're a class act." In the excitement I had forgotten that I was going to retire after this fight.

The scorecards through eleven rounds had me ahead seven rounds to four. But I had no way to know that during the bout.

The crowd of reporters in the dressing room were asking some pretty difficult questions, which I handled as best I could.

The photographers were busy shooting photos of Harrison and myself. Flashbulbs were going off regularly, with their loud, popping sound.

A microphone was put in front of my face.

"Was this fight, revenge for your brother's loss?"

"Yes. I feel I have avenged Billy's only defeat".

"Did Moss hurt you at any time?"

"Look at these welts on my side. Those body shots were painful. Moss is a hellova fighter. I don't know if I could have gone the extra three rounds. I'm glad I didn't have to. Moss is going to be a world champion someday."

"Who's next, champ? A rematch?"

"I don't know right now. I'll probably savor this win for a few weeks and then make a decision. I sure don't want to fight Moss again, anytime soon. But if he wants the rematch, I'll give it to him. He's more than earned it."

"Would Moss have quit if the ref didn't stop the fight?"

"There's no quit in Sam Moss. He's all heart!"

"But Moss couldn't have finished the round," Harrison chimed in.

"What was the difference in the fight that you fought and the one that your brother did, against Moss?"

273

"I won and he lost. I can give you plenty of excuses, the heat being one, and he had a bad cold, but Moss would have beaten him anyway. He was just too big and strong for Billy. Look Bob Harrison gets full credit for this win. It was his strategy, using the crouch in the early rounds that probably saved me some broken ribs and let me keep the title."

"How does it feel to have your first fighter be your first world champion?" someone asked Harrison.

"I feel like a million bucks. Wish that was the purse". Bob responded. The press laughed.

"And, we won this fight the way Billy would have wanted us to win it, clean, with no fouls", I chimed in.

"How did Harrison train you for the fight? Was it the same as Paulie did with Billy?

"No. Paulie was the best. I was lucky to have found the second best, who without any previous training experience allowed me to keep my title. Still, I want to dedicate this big win to Paulie, who I know is at home listening to it. Except for the crouch I trained pretty much the same way as Billy did.

"Will Harrison continue as your trainer?"

"I sure want him too, but obviously it has to be his call. I think if he sticks with it, he's going to be a world class trainer in a very short period of time. Hell, he already proved that he is!"

They turned to Bob Harrison for a response. He only said that he hadn't really given it any thought, but he would love to continue to train me, if I wanted him to.

The press looked at me again. "I want Bob to train me for the rest of my pro career".

The press asked some more questions, the photographers took more photos, and they all left with their story and pictures. the dressing room was suddenly very calm and quiet.

Still, I knew the victory wasn't quite the same without Billy being in my corner. He was always there, to join with me in post-fight celebration. Now, with this title defense, I realized how much I really missed him. But I knew that he was still there, watching over me.

"I thought you promised Jodie you'd retire, Tony. Do you intent to continue?"

I had forgotten. "I'd better talk it over with Jodie before I make that call".

Bob Harrison and his wife Jeanette, joined Jodie and Mary. She had decided to watch her first fight this evening. It was a post fight celebration, which lasted through the night. The Harrison's had gotten a baby sitter for all their children.

We wanted Paulie to join us for a second celebration when we returned to Philadelphia, but he was already gravely ill.

Paulie was on his last legs, and we all knew it. Paulie, who had gone back to drinking but had pretty much stopped eating and was mostly skin and bones. Still it would have been great to have him join in the celebration, an honor that he richly deserved. I presented him with my championship belt in his bed.

This was to be the last time I saw him alive. Paulie died a few days later. The police reported that he had shot himself, a suicide. Maybe it was, but he also could have an outstanding unpaid debt with the bookies. I guess that's one thing that I'll never know.

The fight with Sam Moss provided the biggest purse I would ever have, and set the entire Petrovic family up for a very comfortable retirement at year's end.

Sam Moss never asked for the rematch, and that was probably a good thing for my body. His body shots that night caused some pain and a lot of black and blue welts on my ribs and stomach for many days after the bout. I was pissing blood for about a week.

When I hung up my gloves for good at year's end, which is what we decided upon. It was Sam Moss who won the box-off to become the new middleweight champion of the world, a title he defended with honor many times over.

But, I still had to keep the promise I made to finish the year, and there was still time enough to earn a few extra bucks in a few non-title defenses.

I let Bob Harrison hand pick my opponents, guys that he knew I could easily beat, which I did.

My last fight was on Dec. 12, 1949, at the Philadelphia Coliseum, and I was awarded an easy unanimous decision win. I finished my career with a record of 63-1-2 with one no contest. During that span I had scored 47 knockouts but less than 10 of the one punch variety.

The FBI, along with the Charleston Police Dept., about three months after Billy's murder, tracked down the killer. He turned out to be one of the leaders of the Charleston chapter of the Klu Klux Clan. After a long and much publicized trial, he wound up spending the rest of his life in jail.

Chapter IX

In 1950 I finally hung up my gloves for good.

The World that was all too weary from WWII now faced another problem, as the leaders in North Korea, with the backing of the regime in Communist Chinese, invaded their fellow Koreans in the South. Our involvement in this effort was greeted with mixed reactions, but we had pledged to defend South Korea. Instead of a war, this was called a 'police action'.

I was much too old for the draft, and I thought seriously about joining up to help the troop morale by becoming a boxing instructor for our fighting men.

The problem was that although I had enough money, I had two families to feed, and Jodie was not in favor of me going. She wanted me to finally be able to spend some time with her and the kids. She deserved this family time that she had missed when I was on the road training and fighting.

So the thought of lending a hand to our war effort quickly disappeared from my mind.

Besides, I had also promised Jodie that I was giving up boxing, and this was still boxing related. I just wanted to do my part and lend a hand to those risking their lives to keep us free.

I know that Jodie would have understood if I had gone. We both love this Country and always have. Her family, like mine, was very patriotic.

But now it was time to take care of family business, so as much as I would have liked to volunteer and do my share, I had far too many obligations at home.

Also in 1950, a paranoid, alcoholic US Senator from Wisconsin, Joseph McCarthy, started a nationwide scare by calling many Americans, including those in high places in politics and the arts, Communists.

In truth, he did find a few card carrying members, but most of those he accused where very good people and had their names dragged through the mud for no reason, other than McCarthy's own political enrichment. But I can still remember well those televised hearings.

Although I had retired from the ring in 1950, boxing, which has remained in my blood till this day, was still going strong without me, as Jersey Joe Walcott won the heavyweight title from Ezzard Charles.

Looking back, I still keep thinking, how much better the competition was in my day. How much hungrier and more dedicated the fighters were then. Now, they fight as little as possible and some make more money in one fight than myself and many others made in my entire career. Jealous? Of course not. Money went a lot farther when I was fighting.

But the days when fighters fought 50-100 fights or more before retiring are long gone. I know for sure that no one will ever break Archie Moore's record of 143 knockouts in a career.

Retirement was not very easy for me to adjust to. I was just too darn young, and energetic. Although I know that I didn't have to retire, I had given Jodie my word and that's all that mattered.

I did get quite a few offers to come out of retirement for some very big paydays, but I turned them down. A promise is a promise.

I didn't like to just sit around the house all day, doing little to nothing, except playing with Billy and Tony Jr. and watching TV. This was the lifestyle of a much older man. I took the two boys to a Philly baseball game from time to time, and tried to get them interested in sports via the local YMCA.

I really didn't want to own a restaurant, as a lot of people warned me how hard it was to make a living in that business and about a lot of food that no one had eaten going to waste. After a bit of research, I found out they were all telling me the truth, that it was a hard business to keep going.

I will freely admit that I loved the adoration of the fans and the roar of the crowd, and all the excitement that went with boxing. I think that I missed that far more than the money it brought in. I also missed just being inside the ring and staring down my opponent. I guess I missed all the action. But my word was my bond and to me business was never done with a contract, just a look in the eye and a shake of a hand.

God, do I miss Billy and Paulie and Uncle Johnny. I think of them often and I know I'll be joining them soon, in the big boxing ring in the sky.

One day I called a family meeting (Bob Harrison and his wife Jeanette had now become a part of my family) and we decided to open up the Petrovic Brothers Bar and Grill. And I told Bob that he was in for 1/3. He wanted to put in his share of the money, but I didn't want anything more from him than his friendship, that he had gladly given freely over the years. I trusted him completely, he was always in my corner when I needed him.

At first I wanted to name the bar "Paulies" after my old friend, the man who trained and brought Billy and I to the top of the boxing ladder, but he had recently passed away. Besides the name Petrovic would bring in more customers than "Paulie's". It was the last name of two world champions.

Harrison understood the loyalty I felt to my late trainer, but convinced me that it made far more sense naming it after Billy and me, because I would always be around to greet the customers, take pictures and sign autographs. That was what I felt I needed to remain in the limelight, which for most ex-boxers, fades all too quickly. I really feel that's one of the main reasons that many fighters fight past their prime today, much more so than the money, is the adoration of the fans.

Of course Billy was no longer with us, but we all knew that he would remain part of our family forever. And we had plenty of fight pictures from all of the fights, of Billy, Bob Harrison and myself, adorning the walls of our little establishment.

I started attending college at the University of Pennsylvania, part time, majoring in business. I was determined to keep the promise I made to mom and Uncle Johnny to get a college education, although financially I certainly didn't feel any need for it. I decided to have journalism as my minor, so when I was ready for it, I could do what I am doing now, writing my memoirs in a (hopefully) sensible way. I doubt that I could have put this story together without taking the required courses needed, in college. It was also a way to keep busy.

The three gals, Jodie, Mary and Jeanette worked at the bar, taking turns doing the cooking and ringing up the money on the old black Remington Rand cash register, and waiting on the tables. On their time off, they had to take turns to baby sit all the fast-growing kids. Bob and I did the welcoming duties to all our guests. The business was pretty successful, and we actually turned a nice profit the first year, but the real excitement was gone. The excitement I was missing could only come from stepping through the ropes and into the boxing ring.

Sure, Bob and I signed autographs, and took photos with the guests when they asked us to, but it was far too boring for a guy like me. I was not yet twenty-eight years old. Simply put, although I enjoyed the adoration of the fans, and although the business was successful from the get-go, I found it quite boring. The actual ring action was missing. I wanted to be in the ring and if not that, at least at ringside. I know it may sound a bit barbaric, but I needed to see blood and smell the sweat.

One day, Bob called me aside and said that he really needed to speak to me. I was hoping it wasn't bad news. We went into the business office, which was part of the bar.

"What's up, Bob?" I sat on the edge of the wooden desk and motioned for him to sit down. Bob remained standing.

"I don't know how to tell you this, Tony. You've been really great to Jeanette and me. You're family."

It sure was beginning to sound like bad news. "Come on Bob, spit it out. Since when do we have any secrets from each other? I asked.

"We don't, Tony, and that's the reason why I needed to talk to you right now."

"Sounds pretty serious, what's up?"

Bob finally pulled up a wooden chair and sat down.

"I've had an offer to train and manage an up and coming fighter from Wilkes Barre. He was a Silver Medalist in the last Olympic Games and he's going to be a world champion. I sure don't want to leave you high and dry. You guys have been great to us. But to tell you the truth, I really miss the action. I just don't think I can give the time I need to be here to earn my keep."

I smiled, "I miss boxing, too, Bobby, what's the kid's name?"

I had become lax in following the amateur fighters although I was still following the pro game closely. I know that I really shouldn't have ignored the amateurs. I had always donated money to the local PAL and CYO. I got my start as an amateur and I felt like I owed them a huge debt that I'd never be able to repay. So I donated money to the Police Athletic League, the Catholic Youth Organization, and other worthy groups that helped the kids. But I really wasn't following the amateur fighters at all.

"The kids name is Larry Jordan. He's a raw talent and his current manager and trainer haven't done justice by him. He's only had three pro fights and won them all by close decisions. He should have won all of them easily. He's developed a lot of pretty bad ring habits, so I offered to help."

"I don't know that name. I guess I must be slipping. You're not really going to steal someone else's fighter? I know you better than that," I asked in disbelief.

"No, of course not, Tony", he grinned. "You _**do**_ know me way better than that. I may have been a bit dirty in the ring, but that was then. Now it's first class all the way. The kid has fulfilled his contractual obligation with his team. Obviously he wasn't satisfied. Can't blame him, they wasted his time and. did a lousy job. That's why he called me. It may cost me a few bucks to buy out his contract from his mangers, but I think it's a solid investment.

I scratched my head. "So, are you going to train him?"

"I really want to, Tony, I know that I can make him a champion, but I sure don't want to leave you guys out in the cold. The way business is here; we never seem to have enough help as it is. And you know that you are my best friend. I just don't know what I'm going to do. Look, I owe you. I'll take your advice and do whatever you say. If it's no, I'll call the kid right now and no hard feelings."

I shook my head. "You don't owe me a thing! Tell you what, Bob. Suppose you and I both take the job. You would be the trainer, I'll be the manager, and we keep this business going, even if we have to hire some extra help from time to time. I've also been itching to get back into boxing."

A broad smile slowly crossed Bob Harrison's face. "Thank you, Lord. I was hoping you'd say that, Tony! It will almost be like old times, huh? Just you and me," he asked.

"You bet Bob. And this time, I won't have to get hit to earn a living in the sport. And Jodie won't complain either, because she wont have to worry about me getting hurt."

Bob and I also briefly discussed the possibility of becoming promoters, but we both agreed that was much more work than either of us wanted to handle at that moment. We really didn't care for the politics involved at that end of the business.

But we did leave that option open as a possibility further down the road.

First, of course, we had to talk to our wives and Mary as well, since she certainly was a major part of the family and the business. The gals objected at first, because they had more than enough work to do at the establishment without losing Bob and I. But we quickly assured them that the management end wouldn't take that much time away from the business. Bob would do the actual training, and would hire assistant trainers and only work with the fighters (we also had decided to get ourselves a few other prospects to work with) when time allowed, and of course at all the fights.

The gals remained very hesitant, but once we convinced them that it would benefit all of us financially, and help Bob and I emotionally, it was mutually agreed upon. 'Harrison and Petrovic Boxing' was formed.

Larry Jordan was to be our first project. Bob was right! Whoever was training him after the Olympics didn't do justice to him at all. This guy, a medalist at welterweight in the Olympics, had all the talent in the world, but judging by what I first saw of him training, I knew immediately that this kid had been allowed to develop some very bad habits. I was wondering who trained him so poorly, and why? I have since found out that it was a new group, who brought his contract, but who decided to handle the training end themselves, knowing little or nothing about that end of the business.

Bob and I then purchased the South Side Gym, from the same stupid bigots who bought it from Paulie. Although they made a decent profit with it, we made it very plain to them that they would not be welcome to either train or even visit there. Revenge was sweet.

We trained Jordan at the gym, and at first Bob Harrison became very frustrated. "Boy did the guys who had this kid last, allow him to develop lousy training habits. He's not lazy, just unschooled. This kid has absolutely no clue about motivation, roadwork or sparring. He throws off the wrong foot, and he thinks that defense is a dirty word." Bob would tell me. It was hard for either of us to understand why they signed this raw but very talented fighter and then let him fall by the wayside.

But their loss was to be our gain, as we realized that Larry Jordan had plenty of potential, but right now was just a work in progress.

Bob Harrison and I were determined to make the changes that were necessary in Jordan's workout regime. We would make this undisciplined kid into a future world champion. He was an outstanding amateur, and there was absolutely no logical reason that we could see that would prevent him from making it all the way to the top as a pro. But we knew it would be a challenge, as habits are hard to break.

Working with Larry Jordan was exactly what the doctor had ordered for Bob and I, the opportunity to stay involved in the sport we loved without having to worry about risking our bodies to ring injuries. With a lot of patience and hard work, we were able to change most of the kid's bad habits. Larry Jordan won the welterweight title three years later, at Madison Square Garden in New York, and became our first world champion.

But Bob and I also knew that we needed more than one top fighter in our stable to stay busy. So we placed an ad in the major East Coast newspapers, for 'fighters who want to win'. It had the desired effect, and suddenly the huge number of fighters that telephoned us and signed up and were coming into the gym overwhelmed us. We expected to have five or six fighters, but suddenly we had eleven.

Many of these young men were troubled, minority kids, who had been members of street gangs. They were without the proper training and discipline that boxing brought. They would probably have wound up either in jail or dead in a few years. The doors to our gym were always open to everyone who wanted to train hard.

The fighters who came through those old wooden doors and up the steps, all knew in advance that any violation of our very strict policies would result in them being barred from the gym for good. It was our way of giving back to the game all the great things that boxing had given to us.

These young men were required to stay completely away from tobacco, alcohol and drugs. It was required to do all the required roadwork and sparring. Any problems with the law could mean immediate cancellation of their membership in the gym. The kids understood the rules, and for the most-part abided by them.

Sure, there were a few troublemakers, who tried to fool us by selling drugs (or trying to) at the gym. But the regulars kids there would keep us informed and the problem was quickly disposed of.

You'd think this hard discipline would discourage a lot of the kids, but we always seemed to have a full gym. We quickly got rid of the troublemakers who really didn't want to learn how to fight anyway. Boxing and the discipline of gym training has always been and always will be a great outlet for a young man's frustrations. Bob even found one kid who was coming up to our gym, not to train, but to sell marijuana. We quickly gave him the heave-ho, and notified the authorities.

Billy Jr. grew up to be a strong young man, who, even though surrounded by boxing people, and having the free benefit of being trained as an amateur by Bob Harrison, decided early in his life to pursue a different venue, in law enforcement. He married in 1977 and I became the uncle to two beautiful girls.

Billy Jr. is now a deputy chief of police in Scranton, PA. I know his dad, my brother Billy, is looking down at him and smiling proudly.

Mary would never remarry, and passed away from a stroke in 1979, joining my brother in heaven, where I know they are happy together again.

Jodie and I had three more children, but only one of the Petrovic siblings wanted to become a boxer. Of course that was probably because only one of the four was a boy, and women's boxing was pretty much unheard of in those days.

Tony Jr. was a fine boy who just didn't like to go through the difficult routines that it took on an ongoing basis, to become a pro boxer. He went to college and is now a district attorney in Harrisburg..

We have no complaints about the girls either, all working mothers who have passed along the proud Petrovic blood line. We're very proud of all our children, although most of them have moved and live far away from us, in different parts of America.

However, Tony Jr. and our three daughters have provided us with many wonderful moments when they come to visit us for the holidays, with their children. Jodie and I are proud grandparents of five fine children.

We try to visit all the kids at least once a year, but it's becoming much harder as we grow old, doing all that traveling.

But I digress. Bob and I took Tony Jr. under our wing and guided him through a long, and successful amateur career, which ended abruptly when he suffered a bad cut on the bridge of his nose. That cut would always open up during his fights, and could have cost him any chance he had to become a winning pro fighter.

So after sixty or so amateur bouts, little Tony, who had by that time grown far bigger than me, decided to opt out of boxing, and play college football, where he became an All-American end and a high draft choice for the Philadelphia Eagles in 1972. After football he got his law degree and opened a practice in Pittsburgh.

With his pro football career ready to start, Tony Jr. married his college sweetheart, and it wasn't long before Tony III and IV came along, sandwiched between one girl, Angela.
But Tony IV was the only one of the boys that has shown any interest in boxing. Maybe someday, he will be another Petrovic world champion?

Jodie is still with me, always by my side, as we grow old, flabby and gray together. The bar/restaurant is long since closed, and was sold for a nice profit. We are enjoying our children and grand children in our Golden Years.

Bob Harrison, angered by the segregation that was going on in the Deep South, became a 'Freedom Rider' in 1962, and disappeared while driving to a rally in Mississippi. No one ever heard from him again. If he was a victim of a racial slaying, I guess we'll never know, because his body was never recovered.

I had lost my best friend, but there was some solace in knowing that he willingly gave his life for a cause that we both believed in, racial equality. Two months after Bob's disappearance I closed the gym, gave Jeanette

Bob's cut of the proceeds and Jodie and I decided to move to Florida and just take it easy.

Bob's wife Jeanette and their daughter Barbara, could have come to Florida with us, I asked and was willing to pay their expenses, but they decided to remain in Philadelphia. They are still alive and well, probably still waiting for Bob's return, and I know they are still carrying on the good fight for equality for all. I know that Bob would be very proud of them.

Like Bob, Jeanette too was a class act. For whatever reason Barbara Harrison, a beautiful young lady, never found her "Mr. Right", and remains single.

So why have I written this book, you ask? Because I feel that I've lived a long and interesting life and I wanted to share it. This book's main intent is to not only interest young men, and today even young women, in what I truly believe is the only true one on one sport around, boxing.

The other purpose is to teach history from the eyes of someone who has lived it, and which I was proud to be part of in my many years on this Earth. I've long believed that the past, if we don't learn the many lessons, from it, will be the future, and that can be very scary.

Not only does boxing build character; (and has its share of them as well) it teaches discipline and hard work. Boxing is an equal opportunity sport. There's no place in it for racial hatred. Boxing inspires confidence, gets the kids off the streets and into the gym. When it comes right down to it, what greater measure of a person is the way he conducts himself, one on one, with only the ref to protect him in the squared circle, when the bell rings?

Boxing has changed a lot over the years, and I'm not convinced it's all for the better. I prefer the 15 rounds, the true championship distance for title fights, than the 12-rounds, made for TV today. They say that less rounds saves lives, but I believe that it's the last mile, the final three rounds, that determines a real champion. Bring back the 15 round fights.

Women boxing has enjoyed a resurgence of sorts, but it's still touch and go as to whether or not it will ever catch on. It depends on the trainers and their patience and ability to re-teach the sport. Most lady boxers today come from kickboxing, which is a lot different then the 'sweet science'.

The standing eight count is relatively new, at least to me, and I have mixed emotions about it. It can save a boxer from serious injury, but it also can prolong a fight and create more chance of that injury happening. Call me neutral on it.

The scoring, I think it was easier in the past, where you just scored the rounds for the winner, but fairer today, as you can deduct points for fouls or knockdowns.

Rusty Rubin

A Federal Commission? I think we all know that nothing good ever happens when the Feds get involved. Boxing like other sports should be able to police itself. Sadly, in all the years the sport has been around, no one has come up with a way to make that happen. The creation of a boxing union might help solve that.

Drug testing? They should be made mandatory for steroids, just as CT scans, MRI's and should be used for all fighters to prevent brain damage. HIV? I'm not convinced that it can't be spread by blood flowing into open cuts, but taking any chances would be a mistake. I think HIV testing should also be mandatory, as a precaution.

Boxers should have a retirement fund as well as medical benefits for themselves and their family. I know it's very costly, and hard to organize, but boxers do not deserve to be treated as second class citizens. They put their lives on the line every time they step into the ring.

Life insurance should also be mandatory for the sake of the fighter's families.

For the fighters of today, ten fights, sometimes less, and they think they're ready for a minor title. Sometimes they actually get that title shot. All those sanctioning body titles are good for the fighters. It gives more kids a chance to win something, but is it good for boxing? I think not. All these titles do is confuse the fans and some of the press as well. What is the answer when

296

asked who the champion is. There are so many of them, how can anyone remember?

All these weight divisions? I know this too offers more opportunity for the youth of today. It sure is confusing to an old guy like me, who was used to only eight weight divisions, and of course only one champion.

Pay Per View? I'm not sure if it helps or hurts. I've seen fights on free TV that makes many of the Pay Per View shows look like rip-offs. Sure I pay the price, I can afford it. But can the young men, looking for someone to look up to, a role model if you will, afford it? If not, will they wind up on street corners, sell drugs or join gangs? I much prefer the days past, when boxing was shown on free TV. Maybe I'm just from the old school. I clearly remember the Gillette Friday Night Fights. Like many of the participants in those days, that too is no longer with us.

Those were the golden days of boxing. My personal views will never change anything. But I do long for the way it was.

In truth, as often as not you can see a great fight on Pay Per View, and sometimes you see a dull fight that winds up with a bad decision. I believe that the matchmakers and promoters do their best to provide the fans with a big bang for their buck, so the fans will return, but no one can control the action when the bell rings. The best fights on paper sometimes are the worse to watch. The fights that don't figure to be exciting can be the ones that keep you on the edge of your seats. That's one of the great things about boxing, you never know what will happen when the first bell rings.

Prejudice? Sure, it was the major factor in Billy's death. It was also the cause of Bob Harrison's death. At one time, many of the best black fighters couldn't get a chance to prove themselves, but it was the nature of those times. Look how many years it took Jackie Robinson to break the color barrier and make the Major Leagues.

Football and basketball also were not willing to give the black man a shot until much later. Jack Johnson and 'Sugar' Ray Robinson, Sam Langford, Joe Gans, Joe Louis and many others were world champions long before that. We still don't have enough minority leaders in sports.

Boxing didn't kill my brother, it was some wild-eyed radical redneck, who needed a place to vent his white hood, cross burning hatred, that killed Billy. That guy, we came to learn afterwards, wasn't even a boxing fan. He didn't know a left hook from a fishhook. Billy just happened to be in the wrong place at the wrong time, and at the wrong end of the outcome.

Ring deaths, sure they happen, but very infrequently, and are noticed more than in most other sports. In boxing, when someone gets seriously hurt or killed, the fight's over and the fans are often left unfulfilled and they remember it.

In team sports, if someone gets hurt, he's taken off the field of play and the game continues, and no one really notices the injury at that time. In truth, I truly believe that boxing is one of the safest sports around.

I know, today we have a number of radical groups like the AMA, wanting to ban boxing because they claim that it's 'cruel and barbaric' or for whatever other reasons they choose. They just don't have all the facts, plain and simple. The bottom line is boxing is a job, and like any job, fighters know the risks before they take it.

Is boxing more dangerous than being an airline pilot, a soldier, a coal miner or driving a taxi? Not even close. Yet the AMA hasn't called for a ban on these occupations. Boxing becomes the scapegoat.

When I was participating, boxing the 'sweet science' as it was called. Then the name of the game was hit and not be hit. The trainers used to teach defense, but no so today. Why? Because the paying public wants to see the big knockout, and they enjoy the fast action, which just happens to go along with the fast pace of today's society.

A defensive fighter, a southpaw and a counter-puncher have little market value in today's fight game. Defensive skills aren't taught much because the fans don't want to see defensive fighters, whom they find boring. Southpaws are always avoided because of their unorthodox style.

Fixed fights? I remember what Uncle Johnny told us, but in truth, other than that one incident when Paulie set me up, I never was asked or offered any money to go into the tank (take a dive). I'm not saying it doesn't happen, but if it does, I've never seen it. Billy or Bob Harrison had seen this, they never mentioned it to me. There is a difference between fixed fights and bad decisions. Sure, like everyone else, I've seen more than my share of bad or hometown decisions, which were absolutely absurd. All that proves is that the judges were having a bad day, or listening to the crowd, not that they were paid off.

While make-up of boxing today has changed from mostly poor white folks who needed to make a living, to a multi-racial sport dominated by minorities. They hopefully will find their way out of the ghetto with the money they make. I think that's a very positive thing. It's nice to know you can be competitive and make as much or more money than you can by standing on the street corner selling drugs.

Should athletes be role models? Boxing, like most sports, is a microcosm of our society. You will find some guys like Evander Holyfield who make great role models. While others, like Mike Tyson, whom you wouldn't want your child to spend ten minutes with. OK, I'd trust him more than Michael Jackson, but those types of athletes can be found in all sports.

Are guys like Mite Tyson good for boxing? Yes, because they are unpredictable, they can create a lot of fan interest. Let's face it, the cave man ferociousness puts asses in the seats. Tyson may be good for the business aspect of boxing, but guys like this can cause only damage to a sport which already had a very poor image.

But even more than that, looking back over my almost eighty years of life, I would probably never be able to make the money, and meet the wonderful, mostly blue-color folks that make up all aspects of the sport. Sure, boxing isn't perfect. There are always going to be a few low-lives at or near the top who will try to take advantage and ruin it for the 99% of the decent people in the game.

As boxing changed, so did our society. A world which was at peace when I was born has now become a world of constant and changing danger. Progress does not always work out for the best. I've seen plenty of changes in my 80 years, from President Warren Harding when I was born to George Bush Jr. who leads our Country at present.

I've been around long enough to see the assassinations of many great leaders, like Ghandi, John F. Kennedy, Bobby Kennedy, Martin Luther King, just to name a few, as well as a few thankfully unsuccessful assassination attempts.

I've been around long enough to see the destruction of our Pacific Fleet at Pearl Harbor in 1941, and lived through the cowardly attacks on the World Trade Center in New York on Sept. 11, 1991, almost 50 years later. To this day, I can't figure out why these terrorists don't like Americans. The best answer I can come up with is that we have something they're jealous of, freedom, something that their fanaticism will never allow to happen in their culture.

The slow pace of the society when I was born, has sped up enormously over the years. When I was growing up there was prohibition, and although it never stopped people from drinking, it was felt to be important at the time. Now we can drink freely again, but some folks seem to have graduated to hard drugs, and that's certainly not an improvement.

I've seen the airplane evolve into the jet plane and then the SST. The first man to walk on the Moon was executing. These things we never thought were possible less than 50 years ago. Yes, I've seen the space shuttle disasters as well.

The airplane is now used not only to carry passengers at great speed, but is also used as a weapon of war and mass destruction. Will the same thing happen to our space program? Can Star Wars really happen? I hope not, and if it does, I don't want to live long enough to see it. At my age, I'm relatively assured of that.

The gangs of youths who at one time roamed the streets of the inner city of Philadelphia, rarely did more than rob you or gave out an occasional beating. Now I seem to constantly read about gang killings and drug and turf wars on a regular basis. It's not what I call progress. The Indians had it right from the get-go, no one owns the land, water or sky.

If all these changes happened in just 80 years, what's going to happen in the next 80. I'm pretty sure that the world will continue to change. But it will survive, and I'm grateful that I won't be around to see it, if the moral decay continues at this pace. It would be nice to say that I really believe that I had left this old world a far better place than I found it. Life was much simpler then. While there have been many improvements, sadly I cannot honestly make that statement.

I don't have a crystal ball, and I have absolutely no clue where I'd be today if it wasn't for boxing and the people in the sport that guided me all the way to the top. I can easily say that the sport of boxing made a better man out of me.

No one can ever know that when you go down your chosen path, what events would have happened if you had chosen a different one? It could have been better, but it could also have been far worse. I have boxing and the great boxing folks I met in my lifetime to thank for who and where I am today. Except for Billy's cold blooded murder, I wouldn't change a thing. Even Billy's murder showed me for the first time, the ugly face of racial hatred and I learned from it, as I also did from Bob Harrison's disappearance many years later. I learned that hate is an ugly four letter word.

The many friends I've made from boxing will always be with me. I've lost many of them, which always is part of growing old, but the ones I had from the start, well, we're always there for each other now, because boxing is the greatest fraternity I know of. I have to believe we will be together again in the big ring in sky in years to come.

I belong to a branch of the Veteran Boxers Association, and we meet in Miami every month to tell stories and share personal news and of course to talk about boxing. Most of the stories have changed over the years. The names and rules governing the sport of boxing has changed, but the fraternity remains strong.

No, I never made it into the Hall of Fame. While that would have been a great honor, that in no way changes my feelings for those in the sport of boxing. I understand that I've come close to being selected the past few years, and maybe that's a good omen. But more probably, if I do get in, it will be sometime after my death. Jodie and Tony Jr. can proudly accept the award for me.

Simply put, I've led a good, long life and have absolutely no regrets. I have a clear conscience, and, my memory, while dulled, remains intact. If I hurt anyone in my travels, except for inside the boxing ring, it certainly was never intentional. I'm willing to match my reputation for honesty against anyone who has ever been in this business. I believe that most people in this business of boxing can say the same.

I can and do attribute everything I have today, which is an awful lot, from the many lessons that I learned, to the sport of boxing. The greatest sport in the world!

About the Author

Honesty and loyalty are the two traits that Rusty Rubin values most, and he imparts this in the lead character of *Off the Canvas*.

In his five decades in boxing Rubin has been the sports editor of Ahora Spanish news, managing editor of Nevada Boxing, Ring Arts, Ringsports Magazine and now Ringsports.com the magazine and website.

He founded "RABBIT: a big brother program where fighters go into the jails and get the inmates interested in the sport of boxing. Not getting the needed support it closed down in 1984.

He founded and operates Glove2Glove, a non-denominational prayer group that aids those fallen warriors and their families in need by sending prayers and mail.

Among his awards are IBF Boxing Writer of the Year in 1993, AAIB Boxing Editor of the Year in 1991. He was the only non-Californian inducted into the Bay Area Boxing Hall of Fame (1996) and in 2002 was inducted into the Northwest Boxing Hall of Fame.

Printed in the United States
20596LVS00003B/46-195